KU-158-921

Contents

Foreword

In the early 1990s I can recall a visit to Camp Hill prison on the Isle of Wight, observing a wing, where I was shocked to discover over 50 vulnerable prisoners, all suffering from forms of mental disorder, without any form of psychiatric oversight or constructive day care programme. They were abandoned and destitute within the prison regime with no crossover planning at the point of release to community mental health teams that might make them feel safer or more protected. Today, in Camp Hill and many other prisons, following the NHS's new responsibility for prison healthcare centres and the introduction of in reach mental health services funded by primary care trusts, we are beginning to see the development of a care programme approach, which provides a more consistent framework for those prisoners and others caught up between the systems of mental health and criminal justice.

Whilst awareness and publicly funded programmes of intervention for mentally disordered offenders at the complex interface between mental health and criminal justice have improved over the past decade, in terms of diversion from the criminal justice process, and more focussed responses by community mental health teams and the greater availability of secure beds in special hospitals, there remain gaps in services from the point of arrest of people with mental disorders through to their discharge from prison or hospital.

This edited volume of challenging essays by leading practitioners and academics whose authority, knowledge and expertise competently spans the minefield of complex mental health and criminal justice legislation, particularly since the New Labour government came to power in 1997. The chapters address the gaps in both policy and practice, without ever losing sight of vulnerable individuals, often confused and bewildered, as they pass through the labyrinthine responses of sentencers and professionals, caught themselves between the all too public/political expectations of crime reduction, protecting the public and providing a gateway to treatment services that are ameliorative and sustaining.

The early chapters on the needs of people with mental disorders in police detention and the experiences of vulnerable victims and witnesses give the reader insights into a less familiar territory in terms of public exposure. The case studies illustrate the importance of listening to people's stories, providing protection so that individual rights are not overlooked and respect for those who feel fearful or vulnerable.

The core of the book rests with the law, policy and practice as it relates to mentally disordered people held in detention under some form of psychiatric provision or within the prison system itself. Such is the power of the writing in these chapters that key issues for practice and debate quickly emerge. We see in both forms of detention, parallel themes of concern: the emerging dominance of public safety over the welfare of people with mental disorders, the risks of self-harm and suicide for those detained, over representation of women, foreign nationals and ethnic minorities in prison and secure accommodation, and the marginalisation of family networks of support, often exacerbated by geographical distance making regular contact difficult.

Whilst responses to these concerns are improving in terms of health care planning and better focussed points of intervention, in both prisons and hospitals, surveys reveal that there are hundreds of prisoners, people with mental disorders still languishing in inappropriate prison health centres for want of a bed in mainstream psychiatric provision.

The final chapter, although focussing primarily on risk in the context of probation and mental health practice, chimes with the Government's preoccupation with the climate of fear and the need for greater public protection, even though, in the process, certain groups of offenders, including mentally disordered people with records of sexual or violent offending, may find that the rule of the law, particularly in respect of a fair trial based on evidential proof, is not necessarily a given in the future. In the process, the definition of dangerousness shifts from what you have done in terms of past behaviour to what you might do in terms of the future, as the entry threshold to indeterminate detention. Some further telling points in the chapter suggest that an over obsession with risk technology and the means of enforcement can not only distort aims of treatment, but can serve to estrange the patient from the helper.

Here, the writer along with his fellow writers and editors, gives a timely reminder that whilst we cannot eliminate risk concerns from the agenda of mental disorder in Criminal Justice, the safest response for society, in terms of protection, might be to create a setting where patients/prisoners feel comfortable and respected with a sense of trust in the work of the committed professional.

Professor John Harding CBE,
University of Hertfordshire

About the Contributors

The Editors

Brian Littlechild is Associate Head of School of Social, Community and Health Studies at the University of Hertfordshire, where he has carried out research in the youth justice field on preventive work, ethnicity issues, and restorative justice. He originally worked in residential care, with homeless people, and in a prison aftercare hostel for ex-offenders. He has worked as a social worker in the mental health and child-care fields, and as a manager in youth justice.

He has published extensively on practice and policy issues in the area of young people and mentally vulnerable adults in police detention, and delivered many training courses and conference papers on this.

He is the author of *Police and Criminal Evidence Act 1984: the Role of the Appropriate Adult*: British Association of Social Workers, 1996, and *Appropriate Adults, Appropriate Adult Schemes: Service User, Provider and Police Perspectives*: Venture Press, 2001.

Debra Fearns is Senior Lecturer in Learning Disabilities at the University of Hertfordshire, where she has responsibilities for the Joint Degree in Learning Disabilities that incorporates a nursing and social work qualification. She has carried out research into the provision of services and police understanding of the needs of people with learning disabilities who are held in custody, and delivered training and conference papers in this area.

The Contributors

Sally Angus is currently senior lecturer in social work at Middlesex University, having originally trained as a nurse. In the mid 1980s she worked as a volunteer for her local victim support scheme in North London and subsequently took a paid position with them in the early 1990s. Her research interests include children as victims of crime, and restorative justice.

Sally continues to work as an Associate Trainer for Victim Support, and is a member of their working group which is developing a service for child victims of crime.

Rob Canton is Principal Lecturer in Community and Criminal Justice Studies and Head of the Diploma in Probation Studies Programme at De Montfort University, Leicester. He worked in the Probation Service for many years and has experience of practice, research and training in working with mentally-disturbed offenders.

Steve Cloudsdale is Senior Lecturer in Mental Health Nursing at the University of Hertfordshire. His interests include the ethics of mental health interventions, and post-traumatic stress disorder. He is programme tutor for the BSc Mental Health Studies. His background is in work with substance abusers and those in need of non-residential day care.

John Harding, CBE , is a Visiting Professor in Criminal Justice Studies at the University of Hertfordshire, a member of the Parole Board, Chair of Addaction, a major drug and alcohol treatment agency in the UK, a trustee of the Youth Advocates programme in the UK and the USA, and a council member of the Centre for Crime and Justice Studies. He was the Chief Probation Officer for Hampshire and the Isle of Wight (1985–1992) and for Inner London (1993–2001).

Soo Lee has a background in mental health nursing and NHS management. She was a member of the Mental Health Act Commission and Code of Practice Review Group. Currently she serves as a member of the Mental Health Review Tribunal. She is an active researcher in mental health practice.

Alice Mills is a Lecturer in Criminology at the University of Southampton. She previously taught at Cardiff and the Open Universities and worked for the Social Exclusion Unit on their report, *Reducing Re-Offending by Ex-Prisoners*. Her PhD examined facilities for prisoners with special needs and her current research interests include prison mental health care, resettlement and prisoners' families.

Julia Warrener is a Senior Social Worker at Kneesworth House Hospital, on a medium secure unit for those with a diagnosis of personality disorder. Julia is seconded from this post to the University of Hertfordshire where she is researching social work intervention with service users who have a personality disorder diagnosis.

Phil Woods Ph.D. is currently a Senior Lecturer in Mental Health Nursing at the University of Hertfordshire. His research interests include risk assessment and management, violence prediction, forensic assessment strategies, and developing forensic mental health practice. Phil publishes widely in the professional and academic press and is a regular presenter at national and international conferences.

List of Abbreviations

AA	Appropriate Adult
ACE	Assessment Case Management and Evaluation
ASPD	Anti-Social Personality Disorder
ASW	Approved Social Worker
CPN	Community Psychiatric Nurse
CPS	Crown Prosecution Service
ECHR	European Convention on Human Rights
FCMHN	Forensic Community Mental Health Nurse
FME	Forensic Medical Examiner
GP	General Practitioner
HCR20	Hospital/Clinical/Risk Management 20-item scale
HMCIP	Her Majesty's Chief Inspector of Prisons
HRA	Human Rights Act 1998
MDO	Mentally Disordered Offender
MHA	Mental Health Act 1983
MHAC	Mental Health Act Commission
MHRT	Mental Health Review Tribunals
NHS	National Health Service
OASys	Joint Prison/Probation Offender Assessment System
OGRS	Offender Group Reconviction Score
PACE	Police and Criminal Evidence Act 1994
PCL-R	Psychotherapy Checklist – Revised
PCTs	Primary Care Trusts
PICUs	Psychiatric Intensive Care Units
RMO	Responsible Medical Officer
VPUs	Vulnerable Prisoner Units
VRAG	Violence Risk Assessment Guide

Chapter 1

Introduction

Brian Littlechild

The aims of the book

This book has been written to help fill a gap between two major sets of policy, practice and provision which can appear to be in conflict in terms of aims, methods, and underpinning philosophies. These two are the joint health and social care system, that mainly sets out to support and treat those with mental disorders, and the criminal justice system, that sets out to detect and investigate crime, by dealing with suspects, witnesses and victims.

The book sets out the issues which affect people who have a mental disorder, as defined in the Mental Health Act 1983, when they are caught up in the mental health system primarily as a response to their offending. It also examines the problems and stresses that people with such disorders and mental vulnerabilities experience as a result of this contact with the criminal justice system, including involvement with prison provision and investigative procedures within the criminal justice system. Such investigative procedures include situations where an individual is accused of a crime, or where they are a victim of a crime.

Who this book is for

It is aimed at providing practitioners, managers, legal practitioners, and students in the criminal justice and social care/health systems with a body of information about, and an analysis of, the problematic issues that arise when someone with a mental health or learning disability is caught up within the criminal justice system. It sets out to provide this knowledge in a way that enables professionals and policy makers involved in these systems to provide best practice and services for those with vulnerabilities due to their mental disorder, and highlights the current inadequacies within the current systems.

The book is intended to contribute to breaking down the barriers between the two systems, which includes lack of knowledge by those in the mental health systems of the criminal justice system, and vice versa. This will then perhaps allow information and analysis of each of the two systems in ways that enable policy makers, managers and practitioners in each of these two important enterprises to understand the key factors in the other. The aim is for those in each of the systems to appreciate law, policy and practice within and between each of these two areas. This knowledge and understanding can then help better mesh together the two systems in order to provide appropriately for the safety and well being of mentally disordered individuals, and also the security of the general public, the latter being an important consideration in policy and practice.

Areas of overlap and conflict within the mental health and criminal justice systems

We know that the criminal justice and mental health/social care systems overlap significantly in relation to the individuals who come into contact with them, yet the two systems have very different approaches, focus and provision. The philosophical and practical bases of each system – the psychiatric system for those with mental health problems who have not broken the law, and the prison system for people sent there because of their offending who have no mental heath problems – can be seen to be in almost total dissonance. The McNaughten test was one of the first attempts to address the central problem that is at the heart of the schism between the two monolithic structures – the extent to which an individual should be held personally responsible for their actions. The courts devised this test in 1843 to try to take account of the ways we should view the relationship between offending and the 'irrationality' of certain people with mental disorders, and for over a century this was the standard for the 'insanity' defence. This ruling attempted to resolve the conflict arising from the way in which the criminal justice system relies on a philosophical underpinning of, and assumption about, the level of rationality within people who carry out criminal acts, with ways to deal with people who are seen to be essentially irrational. The test placed the onus on the defence to demonstrate the causal link between mental disorder, as we now term it, and the crime the person is being tried for (Feldman, 1977). The 'insanity' defence was diluted by the introduction of the Homicide Act in 1957, although earlier legislation was preparing the way for this (Harris, 1999; Gunn, 1991) and the term 'diminished responsibility', implying a gradation of rationality rather than an absolute standard, became the key feature in such judgments concerning an individual's culpability for their behaviour and actions, and therefore their rationality. Harris has argued that this has not necessarily provided easy answers to the problem, and that:

> . . . *translating these calibrations into law and policy has proved difficult in the extreme . . .*

(Harris, 1999: 12)

Harris (1999) has argued that the test attempted to place 'unreason' within what has been described as *'the iron equation of crime and punishment affirmed by the classical codes'* (Radzinowicz, in Ancel, 1971: vii) with rationality as the basis of socio-legal codes within the West since the Enlightenment which has marginalised the 'insane' to a great extent. However, within the socio-medical discourse on mental health, the debate centres on the level of risk posed by people with mental health problems whether they have also committed criminal acts or not, and the extent to which it is justifiable to detain someone for these reasons against their will. The same issues also come into play where it is suspected that someone who has a mental disorder is claiming to be the victim of or witness to a crime; can they be believed, as they can be seen to be irrational, and therefore be viewed as unreliable witnesses by the courts?

The mental health system has since the last part of the 20th century increasingly moved away from a perspective deriving from ideas of control of dangerousness (Foucault, 1973) towards ideas of treatment and human rights as eventually legislated for within the Mental Health Act 1983. The broad emphasis has been a move away from ideas of individuals' moral culpability as the cause of mental disorder, towards a medical model where diagnosis, therapy and drug treatments have become central features. This movement has also taken the general approach to mental disorder away from the use of large institutions where people were often detained for many years, if not for life, towards treatment in the community. Meanwhile, the criminal justice system has moved away from ideas of targeting disadvantage and dealing with pathology towards an approach that emphasises the moral culpability of individuals, their responsibility for their own actions, punishment, and more recently, ideas of restorative justice (Johnstone, 2003).

There is one area in which the two systems do have similarities, in that both have the potential to incarcerate individuals against their will, albeit from different sets of considerations. This however leads to its own set of complications in decision-making processes and sets of provision; should these be based on ideas of protection of the public (a consideration of both systems), prevention of re-offending (officially the main aim of the criminal justice system as set out in the Crime and Disorder Act 1998, but not of the mental health system); on natural justice; or on the basis of possible further difficulties arising from the person's mental disorder, a consideration of the mental health system, but not of the criminal justice system?

Whichever is at the forefront of the particular decision maker's thoughts, they have a significant impact on the life of the individual involved. Rob Canton in Chapter 9 examines risk assessment and risk management approaches to mentally disordered offenders in relation to community supervision outside of institutions, and a number of areas of concern and examples of good practice within this growing field. The effects of having been placed under the provision of a section of the Mental Health Act 1983 can be even more severe than the effects of sentences within the criminal justice system (see Chapters 4 through to 7). This point famously became clear to the cinema-going public through the performance of actor, Jack Nicholson, in the 1975 film *One Flew Over the Cuckoo's Nest*, based on the book by Ken Kesey (1963), in which the main character, sentenced to prison, feigns mental disorder as he believes he will have an easier and shorter period of incarceration if he persuades officialdom that he is so disordered. On both counts, he was proved very, and tragically, wrong.

However, the mental health system has seen one recent development that blurs these boundaries. The *Mental Health Bill* proposed that those diagnosed with 'dangerous personality disorder' would be able to be detained on the authority of psychiatrist diagnosis, on the basis that they are considered to be at risk at some point in the future. Accordingly, there were plans to introduce this Bill so that it formed part of the Queen's Speech in November of 2004. The provision to detain individuals suffering from dangerous personality disorders has not been removed, despite opposition from the Mental Health Alliance, the Mental Health Act Commission and mental health professionals. The Department of Health states that this will affect one per cent of cases. In Chapters 6 and 7 Alice Mills provides an account of the current provision for such people within a wider discussion of people with mental health needs in the prison system.

The two systems are not only based on different philosophical and policy agendas, but also administrative arrangements; the criminal justice system, including prisons and community punishments, is within the remit of the Home Office, and the psychiatric and social care systems are the responsibility of the Department of Health. Two such large and complex departments will inevitably have difficulties in formulating clear plans and policies for mentally disordered offenders when the differences in approaches are so profound, in addition to the organisational problems such arrangements inevitably involve. The problems in inter-agency provision are explored by Canton in Chapter 9. Such problems can be exacerbated however, by the perception of many services and professionals, that this group of people, because they provide a double risk, are unattractive to work with; there are also concerns that professional or service expertise is focussed within one system, at the expense of the other (Harris, 1999).

The areas of concern

There is a history of concerns, relating to the areas of overlap between the two systems, that traces it roots back to the reason for the development of the McNaughten test mentioned previously. These concerns gained pace significantly as the 20th century progressed. However, whilst this has been almost exclusively focussed on those who have offended, more recently there have been growing concerns about those with mental health problems and learning disabilities who come into contact with the criminal justice system as alleged victims or perpetrators of crimes, as dealt with by Sally Angus in Chapter 3.

Governments were concerned enough to have two major reviews of the law and policy in relation to mentally disordered offenders in the last quarter of the 20th century. In the 1970s, the Butler Committee (Home Office and DHSS, 1975) considered the trial, sentencing and punishment of 'mentally abnormal' offenders, as they were referred to in the report. They found that many prisoners with mental disorder were sent to prison as there was no intermediate provision with lesser levels of security than the special secure hospitals, but greater than the ordinary, open psychiatric hospitals. The Committee advised that there was a lack of resources for such offenders, and recommended that there should be regional secure units in England and Wales in addition to the three, severely overcrowded, special secure psychiatric hospitals available at that time. The report also considered 'undesirable' the notion of combining punishment and treatment.

Subsequently, the growth of forensic services which occupy space between psychiatry and criminal law, has been a major feature in recent developments for such offenders. However, the impact upon prison services is still very much an acknowledged problem, as set out by Alice Mills in her chapters. In addition, the judgments of forensic psychiatrists have often been a contested area, which is not surprising given that they mediate between the demands of the two very different systems as examined in this book, and also make clinical judgments which many would argue are moral judgments. Such judgments are about culpability and rationality in relation to law, and are not just about the individual in question's mental disorder (or lack of it), but also about how this relates to the demands of society as exemplified through its laws, particularly when there is no concept within Western cultures of any provision which fits comfortably between prison and hospital (see e.g. Harris, 1999; Floud and Young, 1981). The provision of psychiatric care and detention, both in terms of the care and rights and best types of treatment for such patients, are examined by Lee and Warrener in Chapter 4, and Lee, Cloudsdale and Warrener in Chapter 5.

The second major inquiry reported in 1993. This Reed Report was a wide-ranging and comprehensive examination of how mentally disordered offenders were dealt with in both criminal and psychiatric provision (Home Office and DHSS, 1993). The Report made over 200 recommendations, including that of the development of 1,500 regional secure unit beds. The Report concluded that mentally disordered offenders should be dealt with outside of institutions and within the community wherever possible, and that security measures should be no greater than that required to deal with the degree of danger presented by the individual. It also stated that services should aim to maximise the opportunities for patients to return to an independent life, and emphasised the need to divert such offenders away from the criminal justice system and into the health and social care systems, a development examined by Phil Woods in his chapter. This aim was repeated in the government's *The Health of the Nation* document (Department of Health, 1992), yet it is an ideal still far from being realised, as Alice Mills makes clear in her chapters. This document's guidance sets out strategies for provision of services to mentally disordered offenders. These include an effective range of secure and non-secure provision; multi-agency assessment and diversion of offenders; and a focus on the mental health needs of transferred and discharged prisoners.

The National Health Service Confederation's report, *No Bars Against Care: Policy Proposals for the Treatment and Care of Mentally Disordered Offenders* (NHS Confederation, 1997) succinctly sets out the deliberations of their panel of experts, and demonstrates that the areas of concern pointed up by the Butler and Reed reports are still very much current and problematic issues. After concluding that there is no coherent legal and diagnostic framework for people suffering from personality disorders and multi-diagnoses (personality disorder, mental illness and substance misuse), and that the range of resources to provide care for patients with complex long-term persistent disorders is insufficient and patchy, the report notes that communication between agencies and their staff about the needs of individual patients is fragmented and poor, especially at the point of discharge from prison or hospital. The latter point is emphasized in relation to the urgent need to build up better multi-agency working practice and policies between the agencies involved.

These matters are at the heart of the considerations of and contributions from the different authors of the chapters in the book.

The contents of the chapters

The chapters examine the main areas of overlap between the two systems, and how policy makers, managers and professionals can consider what is best practice and provision within each of them.

Chapters 2 and 3 examine the problems of mentally vulnerable people who are in contact with the police as victims or alleged perpetrators of crimes, and the types of support available from various professionals and services. Littlechild and Fearns' chapter provides an account of the issues faced by people with a mental disorder or other mental vulnerability when they are detained by the police in connection with a suspected offence. There are a number of issues which arise from the detention of people with mental disorders, both to ensure that they are not disadvantaged by police detention and questioning techniques because of their vulnerabilities, but also to ensure that justice is done if they should have limits and boundaries about criminal behaviour set appropriately within the criminal justice system. These issues for detained vulnerable adults are addressed based on research evidence, case law, and the views of those involved in receiving services designed to support them. Apart from the effects of detention on the person's mental disorder and subsequent well-being, the concerns from the criminal justice system's viewpoint is the risk of false confessions from vulnerable adults arising from their mental disorder and the stress of being held in police detention.

The main problems for people with mental disorder are in having their vulnerability recognised; accessing adequate medical support; and in the provision, and effective practice, of 'Appropriate Adults', as defined in the Codes of Practice (Home Office, 2004) produced under the Police and Criminal Evidence Act 1984.

An account is given of the strengths and weaknesses of the current state of the provision of support services, including the police surgeon or Forensic Medical Examiner, and the sometimes problematic Appropriate Adult role. This latter role is the one that many workers in the criminal justice system and mental health systems are likely to find themselves having to operate – usually with little or no training for this demanding and important role. The effects on vulnerable detainees of police detention, and how practitioners in the criminal justice system and mental health systems can most effectively carry out the role of Appropriate Adults for them, are also covered. The roles of the different professionals who may also be involved are all set out.

In the next chapter, Sally Angus examines those people who are mentally vulnerable but not accused of having committed an offence, those who are on the other side of the investigative process; who are victims or witnesses. The issues that have a particular impact on vulnerable victims and witnesses have for far too long been neglected within the criminal justice system; indeed, victims as a group were marginalised in the whole of the criminal justice system for many years. This has now started to change, but a great deal of work still needs to take place. The chapter sets out the problems and vulnerabilities of victims and witnesses when having to cope with their experience of crime, and then having to cope with the stresses of a system which demands the types of recall and confidence which many people cannot muster even when they have no mental disorder; within police interviews for example, or within cross examination in court, with searching questions from powerful people and sometimes deliberately intimidating lines of questioning.

The chapter explores the types of support in practice and policy, such as set out in the 2002 White Paper *Justice for All*, and the 2002 *Achieving Best*

Evidence Guidance from the Home Office, which have started to change agencies' attitudes and procedures in relation to vulnerable groups. The responses of professionals and supporters that are needed to counteract the disempowering effects victims and witnesses can so often experience are set out. Clear definitions within the legislation concerning who is a vulnerable victim or witness are included, and the types of support they should be able to expect as a result of being so defined, are also set out. Good practice issues are presented in relation to the pressures and intimidation vulnerable victims and witnesses can experience, and also the recent legislation which sets out to deal with these, including the Youth Justice and Criminal Evidence Act 1999, and the Domestic Violence, Crime and Victims Bill 2004.

Chapters 4 through to 7 are then concerned with institutional settings provided by the two systems. Lee and Warrener's chapter sets out the provisions under which people who have committed crimes may be detained in psychiatric provision under mental health legislation. The definitions of mental disorder are discussed, as are the facilities and treatment regimes. The legal rights of such detained people are set out, and the importance of the tribunal system which can arrange release from such institutions, is discussed. The importance of legal representation in these tribunals is emphasised. After this exposition of the law and the legal processes involved in this area, Lee, Cloudsdale and Warrener move on, in Chapter 5, to consider the issues for people who have to live in the different types of psychiatric provision afforded to them, and the effects on their choices, treatment and human rights in relation to their care, and the planning for their future.

These authors propose consideration of Frankena's 'do no harm' model, which emphasises an approach of beneficence as a focus of, and gauge for, patients' (as they then become) care in these circumstances. The effects on patients' privacy, dignity and loss of ability to engage in personal and sexual relationships – in and outside the institutions – are also given careful consideration. Maintaining contact with family and friends is a particular problem, making greater the problems for eventual rehabilitation. The effects of the priority given to security over care and therapy are then set out. The schisms between the mental health and criminal justice systems are also set out, and the potential for misunderstandings about the roles of others in the separate systems, and lack of adequate resources, are highlighted. They also provide a critique of risk assessment and risk management approaches within such regimes, and the nature of gender-related problems in the system, in which women are over represented.

Alice Mills then provides an account and analysis of the prison system in her two chapters. In her first chapter, she explores the experience of mentally disordered prisoners, and the responsibilities of the Prison Service and NHS to care for them, providing a focus for this chapter. As part of such a focus, it also sets out the particular mental health needs and experiences of different minority groups. The experiences of women within the prison system are also considered, as well as those who are nationals of other countries, and where there may be combinations of these factors. Mills considers how vulnerability in prison relates to a mentally disordered offender's mental and emotional state, and their ability to adjust and adapt to prison life.

Calling upon a wide range of policy documents and research findings, Mills critically examines how the Prison Service's statement of purpose, that it has a duty to look after prisoners with humanity and help them to lead law-abiding and useful lives in custody and after release, impacts upon prisoners with mental health problems. Following an exploration of the prevalence of mental disorder, and how this relates to the causes and incidence of suicide and self-harm in prison, Mills discusses the need for prison health care of an equivalent standard to that of the NHS, and the history and current state of affairs of attempts to provide such care. Mills also mentions how issues of ethnicity seem to affect decisions in diversion schemes, which are discussed in greater depth in Phil Woods' chapter. The value and limitations of screening procedures to assess any mental disorder in new prisoners are discussed, and issues of dual diagnosis, as well as a new initiative in mental health provision, Mental Health In-Reach, in which multi-disciplinary mental health teams can play an important role, particularly as many of these prisoners have multiple needs. Assessment should therefore include how to meet such prisoners' mental and physical health needs through appropriate treatment, as well as ensuring that their mental health problems and vulnerabilities are not negatively affected by their imprisonment.

In her second chapter, Mills then focuses on the provision of specialist resources, regimes and practice for dealing with the particular problems arising for prisoners with mental disorder. Aspects of regimes which can exacerbate mental health problems and any associated vulnerability are examined, along with more suitable forms of accommodation for these prisoners. The chapter examines the therapeutic community regime at Her Majesty's Prison (HMP) Grendon Underwood, and the type of prisoners – mostly those with personality disorder – they set out to treat. It also discusses the recently developed 'Dangerous and Severe Personality Disorder' (DSPD) unit at HMP Whitemoor, as it had been recognised that some 1,400 prisoners were at high risk of very serious offending, and likely to be disruptive, although some of them may benefit from therapeutic communities like HMP Grendon.

Mills also looks at the work being undertaken by the close supervision centres at HMPs Woodhill and Durham, which in 1999 were found to contain the extreme end of the 1,400 people with DSPD. These are centres which accommodate prisoners who repeatedly challenge the authorities or commit serious acts of violence, which the Chief Inspector of Prisons has suggested can be used to accommodate prisoners with DSPD, if they are based on a combination of control and treatment, with prisoners receiving mental health assessments, and individual care and management plans being drawn up for each prisoner.

Risk assessment and management procedures for mentally disordered prisoners and those who are vulnerable to suicide or self-harm are then addressed, with analysis of suicide prevention programmes, and also of the First Night in Custody scheme initiatives which start from a recognition that the first 24 hours in custody is a time of increased risk of suicide and self-harm for prisoners. Prisoners' anxieties and feelings of hopelessness can be particularly acute at this time, and they may also be suffering withdrawal symptoms from drugs or alcohol. A range of practical and emotional assistance is provided to support new prisoners and address their vulnerability.

The effectiveness of segregative facilities for prisoners with special needs set up by several prisons is also examined. Many of these prisoners have mental health problems, but they may also have severe drug or alcohol problems, learning difficulties, or physical disabilities which make it difficult for them to participate in active prison regimes, and many tend to be vulnerable to suicide or self-harm, to victimisation by other prisoners, and violent outbursts. Such facilities act as 'halfway houses' between the main prison wings, and generally accommodate between 40 and 50 prisoners. Research quoted by Mills found that such units can help these prisoners to cope with the pressures of prison life. The final part of this chapter then sets out how these prisoners might best be given support and help to resettle into the community.

As mentioned previously, the aim of diverting mentally disordered people from the criminal justice system has been a developing one over the past 20 years. Phil Woods' chapter examines the policy and practice of diversion of mentally disordered people from custody within the criminal justice system. The chapter examines the features of those who are diverted, and those who are not, and what happens to these groups. The differences between the more than 60 schemes within the criminal justice system are set out, within consideration of the recommendations of the Reed Committee, the approaches of the Crown Prosecution Service, and bail and remand practices. The features of effective diversion schemes are set out, as are the problems that can affect them. Examples of several of these schemes are given in detail, as are different models of provision. The roles of professionals such as forensic psychiatric nurses and psychiatrists are discussed, as well as those of forensic medical examiners or police surgeons.

Rob Canton's chapter provides a critical account of the assessment of risk for those offenders within the community who have mental health problems, within a wider critique of the value and limitations of risk assessment procedures as they are applied to this group of people, and the prejudices that affect them. The place of inter-agency working, and the efficacy of the procedures and protocols within such procedures and policies, is examined. The types of issues that are currently taken into account in the relationship between community supervision and mental disorder are examined. Canton argues for careful attention to be paid to the risk factors relating to people with mental health problems offending, and the risk factors relating to the wider populace's offending, otherwise the prejudices against this group can negatively affect assessment of risk for them. The effects of professional judgment-making on the assessment of risk, and how this can affect carefully planned 'technical' means of risk assessment that are designed to eliminate subjectivity as far as possible, are considered, as is who should contribute to such assessments – including, crucially, the service users themselves.

These considerations are set out with special reference to the propensity towards violence from this group. A particular consideration of current models of risk assessment and practices within probation work and psychology and psychiatry relating to predictability and issues of assessment, as well as risk management issues, is provided within this chapter. The 'double mandate' of mental health practitioners – to treat patients as well as to prevent crime – is clearly set out, as are the main forms and tools of risk assessment and management used within each system. Issues of coercion and compliance within the practitioner's role are also considered.

The book, then, provides examination of the treatment of mentally vulnerable people who are suspected of having committed an offence, are being questioned as a victim or witness of an offence, or are incarcerated within a prison department or psychiatric provision. It will give elements of information and knowledge to enable professionals and policy makers to understand the crossover points between the two systems (which can disadvantage those with mental health or learning disabilities) and deal with those problems more appropriately.

The use of the terms 'mentally vulnerable', 'learning disabilities' and 'mental disorder' within the book

There is sometimes confusion in the use of the terms mental disorder and learning disabilities. In one of the areas discussed in this book, where vulnerable people are detained by the police on suspicion of having committed an offence, the Home Office have now moved on from the use of the term 'mentally handicapped', which has been out of use by enlightened groups for a number of years, to 'people with learning disabilities'. *Valuing People* (Department of Health, 2000) states that:

Learning disability includes the presence of:

- *A significantly reduced ability to understand new or complex information, or to learn new skills (impaired intelligence), with;*
- *A reduced ability to cope independently (impaired social functioning); which started before adulthood, with a lasting effect on development.*

The term 'learning disability' is more usual in literature and professional discourses rather than the term 'mental impairment' used in the Mental Health Act 1983.

The Mental Health Act 1983 defines 'mental disorder' in the following ways:

- **Mental disorder** means mental illness, arrested or incomplete development of mind, psychopathic disorder and any other disorder or disability of mind and 'mentally disordered' shall be construed accordingly.
- **Severe mental impairment** means a state of arrested or incomplete development of mind, which includes severe impairment of intelligence and social functioning and is associated with abnormally aggressive or seriously irresponsible conduct on the part of the person concerned and 'severely mentally impaired' shall be construed accordingly.
- **Mental impairment** means a state of arrested or incomplete development of mind (not amounting to severe mental impairment) which includes significant impairment of intelligence and social functioning and is associated with abnormally aggressive or seriously irresponsible conduct on the part of the person concerned and 'mentally impaired' shall be construed accordingly.
- **Psychopathic disorder** means a persistent disorder or disability of mind (whether or not including significant impairment of intelligence) which results in abnormally aggressive or seriously irresponsible conduct on the part of the person concerned.
- **Mental illness** remains undefined within the Mental Health Act (1983) and its accompanying Memorandum, which stated that its operational definition and usage is a matter for clinical judgment in each case. This lack of definition makes it difficult to have a full understanding of what is meant by 'mental illness' and adds to the complexities that professionals face in identifying vulnerable adults and ensuring their rights are protected.

At times in this book, the term 'mentally vulnerable' is used, or 'mental vulnerability', phrases used by the Home Office in its 2004 revision of its *Codes of Practice* issued under the Police and Criminal Evidence Act 1984 (Home Office 2004: Note of Guidance 11C), as discussed in Chapter 2, which relates to people who are held in police detention. The phrase covers those who have mental disorder, and also includes other vulnerabilities that are not so 'clinically' determined within the Act's strict definition. The term is used when there is need to consider those who perhaps do not fit the strict definition of the Mental Health Act 1983 in addition to those who do, such as when people are held in police detention, or where they are victims or witnesses.

References

Ancel, M. (1971) *Suspended Sentence*. London: Heinemann Educational.

DoH (1992) *The Health of the Nation*. London: HMSO.

DoH (2001) *Valuing People: A New Strategy for Learning Disability for the 21st Century*. London: DoH.

Feldman, P. (1977) *Criminal Behaviour: A Psychological Analysis*. London: Bailliere Tindall.

Floud, J. and Young, W. (1981) *Dangerousness and Criminal Justice*. London: Heinemann.

Foucault, M. (1973) *Madness and Civilisation: A History of Insanity in the Age of Reason*. London: Vintage.

Gunn, J. (1991) The trials of psychiatry: insanity in the twentieth century. In Herbst, K. and Gunn, J. (Eds.) *The Mentally Disordered Offender*. Oxford: Butterworth Heinemann/Mental Health Foundation.

Harris, R. (1999) Mental disorder and social order: underlying themes in crime management. In Webb, D. and Harris, R. (Eds.) *Mentally Disordered Offenders: Managing People Nobody Owns*. London: Routledge.

Home Office (2004) *The Police and Criminal Evidence Act 1984: Codes of Practice*. Revised edn. London: HMSO.

Home Office and DHSS (1975) *Report of the Committee on Mentally Abnormal Offenders. (Butler Report)* Cmd 6244, London: HMSO.

Home Office and DHSS (1993) *Review of Health and Social Services for Mentally Disordered Offenders and Others Requiring Similar Services (Reed Report)*. Cmd 2088, London: HMSO.

Johnstone, G. (2003) (Ed.) *A Restorative Justice Reader*. Cullompton: Willan Publishing.

Kesey, K. (1963) *One Flew Over the Cuckoo's Nest*. New York: Signet.

National Health Service Confederation (1997) *No Bars Against Care: Policy Proposals for the Treatment and Care of Mentally Disordered Offenders*. Birmingham: NHS Confederation.

Chapter 2

Mentally Vulnerable Adults in Police Detention

Brian Littlechild and Debra Fearns

Introduction

This chapter provides an account of the problems faced by people with mental disorder and other mental vulnerabilities (hereinafter referred to as people with mental vulnerabilities) when they are detained by the police and suspected of having committed an offence, and how these might best be dealt with. The term 'mentally disordered' is defined in the Codes as having the same meaning as in the Mental Health Act 1983 as:

> ... mental illness, arrested or incomplete development of mind, psychopathic disorder and any other disorder or disability of mind.
>
> (s. 1(2) Mental Health Act 1983, as quoted in Note of Guidance 1G, Code C, Home Office, 2004)

The interpretation of this definition then impacts upon how the services identify and recognise vulnerability. These matters are also discussed within this chapter.

The main problems for people with mental vulnerabilities are having their vulnerability recognised; accessing adequate medical support; and the provision and effective practice of Appropriate Adults (AA). These issues for detained vulnerable adults are addressed using research evidence, case law, and the views of those involved in receiving services designed to support them.

An account of the strengths and weaknesses of the state of current provision of support services is given, including the role of the police surgeon or Forensic Medical Examiner, as they are now often termed, and the sometimes problematic AA role for vulnerable adults. This latter, a demanding and important role, is the one which most workers in the criminal justice and mental health systems are most likely to find themselves having to carry out, usually with little or no training. The effects of police detention on vulnerable detainees, and how practitioners in the criminal justice and mental health systems can most effectively carry out the role of AA for them, are also covered. A number of miscarriages of justice, as adjudged in case law relevant to the provision and practice of AAs are also examined. The Home Office's Code of Practice C, Note of Guidance 11C (Home Office, 2004), hereinafter referred to as the Code and issued under the Police and Criminal Evidence Act 1984 (PACE), which regulates the police's treatment of detainees, states that:

Although juveniles and people who are mentally disordered or otherwise mentally vulnerable are often capable of providing reliable evidence, they may, without knowing or wishing to do so, be particularly prone in certain circumstances to provide information that may be unreliable, misleading or self-incriminating . . . and the appropriate adult should be involved if there is any doubt about a person's age, mental state or capacity.

Apart from the effects of detention on the person's mental disorder and subsequent well-being, the concern from the criminal justice system's viewpoint is the risk of false confessions from vulnerable adults arising from their mental disorder and the stress of being held in police detention.

In addition, the roles of the different professionals who may also be involved, e.g. the solicitor, the police surgeon (now often known as the Forensic Medical Examiner (FME)), the Community Psychiatric Nurse (CPN), and the Appropriate Adult (AA), are all set out.

Vulnerable adults' experiences of police detention

This section is about two people who have experiences of AAs, solicitors and the police whilst detained. Interviews were undertaken with the full and informed consent of each person (Fearns, 2001a; Hansen, 2001a). Their accounts lead into the sections that set out the issues that arise from published work, and case law.

Mike (a pseudonym) has mental health problems, and explained in his interview that he had often been arrested by the police during the previous 30 years (Hansen, 2001a). Mike is generally positive about most of the AAs who have attended for him. His general observations about being detained in police stations are:

It's very intimidating in a police station and as I say I've been going in there years, it's very intimidating. It is very, very daunting. You never get used to it, well, I've never got used to it.

I mean you can be in a police station where you can get railroaded, it does happen. Sometimes if you're in a police station, if you're on your own, they will tend to keep you for as long as they can keep you, you know 24 hours, before they have to get extra time. Then they start firing questions at you – and it's 'oh! well go on then, I must have done it'. It just sounds familiar, so you admit it. I've got quite an extensive record and nine times out of ten I admit what I've done, whether I've done it or not.

Mike has the following observations about the differences between the role of the solicitor and the Appropriate Adult:

The solicitor will just tell you to say nothing. Don't say anything. But I always find if there's someone else there with you then the police won't get up to certain things that they get up to, like keeping on and on questioning you.

I always found that the appropriate adult sort of acts like a solicitor anyway, so I didn't really need a solicitor. I didn't need both of them there. Whereas the appropriate adult more or less come out straight away, more or less. There has never been any problems in terms of long delays in waiting for somebody. With solicitors there is.

Mike would give the following advice to the police about the Appropriate Adult service and to Appropriate Adults themselves:

To listen, and to look up on the rules, I suppose. Stick with them [the detainees], *stick by their side. Because that's the bit, it's very intimidating in a police station.*

Mike also said that he had been detained dozens of times, and was well-known by his local police, yet did not always have an AA called for him.

Ian (a pseudonym) has a learning disability. In an interview with him, whilst accompanied by his care worker, he recounted his experience of detention (Fearns, 2001a). Ian said of his time in the police station:

The police need to have more love and understanding and not be against the person . . . If a person hasn't got a solicitor, they should find someone who has more love and understanding . . . if they are worse than I am, they need someone . . . The custody officer needs to listen people better, and some are ignorant and need to look at attitudes. Asking me to read when it's late and too hard.

Ian had a negative experience of the police and the AA. The police had asked him 'Can you read words?' When Ian shook his head, the officer had said 'You need glasses, then', to which Ian replied, 'I don't, my eyesight is fine'. He was not asked if he wanted anyone he knew to act as the AA. It was someone who happened to be in the police station for some other purpose. Ian said, 'He wasn't very nice, either. I was scratching myself, and the AA said "You've got fleas".' (Ian's support worker who was with him in the interview stated that Ian had psoriasis that made him itch, particularly when stressed.)

It can feel that the police have a monopoly of power in the situation, and lead to a great deal of nervousness and disempowerment not only for the vulnerable person, but also the Appropriate Adult. These experiences can lead to a detainee making statements or being inadvertently led into saying something they do not mean because they feel intimidated by the situation (Littlechild, 2001). The effect of certain questioning practices, deployed in ways which can seriously disadvantage vulnerable detainees, are discussed in the research of Pearse and Gudjonsson (1999).

The notion of vulnerability arising from such vulnerabilities does not fit easily with the normal investigation processes and interviewing styles of the police, which have been developed, in part, to overcome the resistance of non-vulnerable adults (Pearse and Gudjonsson, 1999).

The main points arising from the interviews with Mike and Ian are the need for respect for the detained person; proactive communication from police officers and Appropriate Adults towards people with mental vulnerabilities indicating that they are concerned about the detainee's welfare as well as the investigation of the offence; and the Appropriate Adult taking care to spend time with the detainee, as well as to convey that they are confident in their role as the Appropriate Adult.

The detainee is likely to be feeling a range of different feelings and emotions at the police station. Some of the same types of responses can also be expected in vulnerable witnesses and victims (see Chapter 3). The detainee may be feeling:

- Claustrophobic.
- Hungry or thirsty.
- Fearful, disempowered or intimidated, resulting in them being prone to agree to anything suggested to them just to gain release from detention.
- Distressed about lack of privacy, dignity or opportunity for religious observation.
- Impelled towards self-harming or suicidal behaviour.
- Excited by the situation, even possibly enjoying the attention: this may particularly be the case for some people with learning disabilities.
- Paranoid: is the person avoiding eye contact? Might they be seemingly distracted by listening to voices only they can hear?
- Concern about medication not being available.
- Relieved, if they have been feeling guilty about something else they have done.
- Confused about what is going on and why; they may not comprehend the terms and expressions being used.
- Anxious about cultural issues, relating to dress, diet or washing.
- Just plain worried, anxious, stressed, scared, ashamed, or angry.

Some detainees wish the professional in their AA role to 'rescue' them; the AA needs to set out limits and boundaries of the role, as well as reassuring the detainee about what the AA can and cannot do.

Some people with vulnerabilities will have learnt that the police will not proceed against them if the suspected crime is relatively minor, as the time and effort of the police in dealing with people with vulnerabilities can be considerable.

Identifying mental disorders

The police have a duty to call an AA where a suspect of any age appears to be mentally disordered or otherwise mentally vulnerable, or where they appear to be a juvenile (under the age of 17) (Home Office 2004: paragraphs. 1.4–1.5).

However, the research evidence suggests that only between two per cent (Robertson et al., 1995) and seven per cent (Gudjonsson et al., 1993) of detainees have a mental illness. Research relating to people with learning disabilities, carried out by Gudjonsson et al. (1993) found that three per cent of detainees in their sample required an AA.

It is acknowledged that the police lack specialist expertise and training in recognising when someone's mental health or learning disability is putting them at a disadvantage in detention and interview (Palmer and Hart, 1996); and when, or if an FME, CPN or AA is required (Pearse, 2001). Custody officers are managing an often hectic and sometimes threatening environment, and can find it difficult to find an appropriate room or the time needed to assess the mental state of the detainee, even if they have been fortunate enough to have been given the skills to carry out such an assessment. Palmer and Hart (1996) found that it is usually the police or solicitors who first recognise that a detainee may have a mental disorder, but that this is rather a hit-or-miss process. They found that, in the absence of specific training on mental disorder, police were alerted to this in two main ways; being informed about it by others (e.g. family, voluntary groups, social care professionals), or perceiving it themselves, usually from how the detainee looked or behaved. Both approaches are too unsystematic and open to chance.

Palmer and Hart's research (1996) found that custody officers were uncertain about how to identify adults within the vulnerable groups:

There is no test as far as I can work out. It would be easy if you could put them on the equivalent of a breathalyser machine and come out with a result, but it doesn't work that way.

It would be difficult to put into words how you would recognise those signs.

I sort of look for a person's demeanour and behaviour.

They might even have a physical appearance of appearing mentally ill.

I'm not trained, so I can only go on intuition, personal feeling, how I feel about that particular thing.

There were particular problems for officers distinguishing between mental health problems and learning disabilities. One court diversion worker (see Chapter 8 on court diversion schemes) stated that:

The parts of PACE on mental health are very fuzzy.

. . . and two custody officers between them stated:

It's over my head, I'm afraid.

There is no definition under PACE. It comes down to, I think, judgment by the officer in the case.

Everybody's presumption of mental disorder is different.

They found that similar means of identifying detainees with vulnerabilities were used by solicitors.

Fearn's research (2001b) also found that custody officers frequently use 'rule of thumb' approaches, and the main signals they looked for to recognise vulnerability were appearance or demeanour, erratic or unusual behaviour, and lack of ability to read and write, or to understand what is being said to them. She found that there was confusion in officers about identification particularly in relation to learning disabilities, for example in distinguishing between this and mental illness, and in assessing reading and writing skills as a method of identification. It also appeared that they would recognise florid, psychotic behaviour relatively easily, but not other signs, nor know how to assess a person if they did not show behavioural evidence of mental disorder.

The custody officer is charged with ensuring that a detainee receives appropriate attention as soon as possible, whether requested by the detainee or not, if they:

- Appear to be suffering from physical illness.
- Are injured.
- Appear to be suffering from a mental disorder.
- Appear to need clinical attention (Home Office 2004: paragraph 9.5).

There are specific requirements for the police in relation to their duty to recognise mental vulnerability and to take this into account when considering interviewing a detainee. Code C states that 'Before a detainee is interviewed, the custody officer, in consultation with the officer in charge of the investigation and appropriate health care professionals as necessary, shall assess whether the detainee is fit enough to be interviewed' (paragraph 12.3), and determine what safeguards should be put into place. Interviews cannot normally go ahead if they will cause significant harm to the detainee's physical or mental state, or if anything the detainee says might be considered to be unreliable in subsequent court proceedings because of the detainee's physical or mental state (Home Office 2004: paragraph 2, Annex G). The appropriate health care professional should advise on the need for an Appropriate Adult to be present, if reassessment may be necessary after a period of time, and should take into account functional ability, and not just medical diagnosis (Home Office 2004: paragraphs 4 and 5, Annex G). The appropriate health care professional will identify and quantify risks; inform the custody officer if the detainee's condition is likely to improve; will require or be amenable to treatment; and indicate how long it may take for such improvement to take effect. These considerations and recommendations will be set out in writing as part of the custody record (Home Office 2004: paragraph 6, Annex G).

Mike's account of his detentions highlights how even someone attending a police station regularly and well-known as having a mental disorder may not always have an AA called. It also highlights that police systems and computer records are not necessarily helpful in ensuring the vulnerability of a detainee is addressed, even when known to the police. Effective recording on police computers would help remedy this, particularly if held on the National Police Computer records, but there are a number of problems about legislation on data protection and its interpretation in local police forces to be overcome; see for example the *Observer* of 21 December (*Observer*, 2003), concerning passing of information between police forces on Ian Huntley, in relation to the factors which had a part to play in the lead up to the murders of Jessica Chapman and Holly Wells. Another problem would be to protect the rights of those who have been previously identified, so they do not have such identification acting against them, leading to prejudicial labelling.

For a detailed discussion of these problems and how recognition might be improved, see Gudjonsson et al. (1993), Hansen (2001b), and Fearns (2001b).

Even when adults with vulnerabilities were identified, an AA was often not called, due partly to confusion about who determined the need to call one, but also confusion as to whether the AA was needed for 'minor' offences (Palmer and Hart, 1996; Bean and Nemitz, 1995).

In attempting to remedy this problematic state of affairs, in the 1990s the Metropolitan Police introduced a system of screening questionnaires to help officers to improve assessment and aid identification of people from the vulnerable groups. Such checklists might include, for example, whether the detainee had been to a relevant special school, was in contact with a social worker or community psychiatric nurse, was taking any medication, or had received treatment from a psychiatrist or psychologist; methods found to be used by some custody officers in Palmer and Hart's study in South Yorkshire (1996). Clare and Gudjonsson's (1992) suggestion was to include questions on the custody record that would encourage the detainee to give information that would help alert the police to such vulnerabilities, including whether the person themselves believed that they thought that they had any need for special protection. Palmer and Hart suggest that the custody officer should specifically ask the arresting officer if there was any reason to suppose the detainee might need an FME or AA.

In general, those who have an IQ at or below 70 are viewed as learning disabled, whilst those with an IQ between 100 and 71 are sometimes viewed as borderline learning disabled. People with learning disabilities will often not reveal this to the police, believing this is private information, compounding the problem for the police in trying to recognise this group. Quite often, the police will determine that someone is learning disabled if they cannot read, or have attained poorly in their education, which may or may not be the case.

PACE, under section 77(3), expressly includes 'significant impairment of intelligence and social functioning' in its definition, and in the case of Silcott, Braithwaite and Ragnip (1991) the judge indicated that the issue of 'mental handicap should be looked at broadly' (quoted in Palmer and Hart, 1996: 36).

The roles and responsibilities of the different professional groups

The following section contains description and analysis of the roles and responsibilities of different professional groups, and inter-agency working, during police detention and interview, as it is important to have knowledge and understanding of who has responsibility for what during the detention and the interview.

The custody officer is the key police officer in any detention. They have the role of ensuring the provisions of the Police and Criminal Evidence Act 1984 Codes of Practice are upheld; they are personally responsible for this, and can be disciplined if they fail to do so. They are responsible for initially determining if the detainee is mentally disordered, learning disabled or otherwise mentally vulnerable, and for the proper treatment of the detainee from the moment of arrival at the police station through to the time of their release, bail or being taken to court. They are not involved in the investigation of the offence.

If the Codes are broken to such an extent that the Crown Prosecution Service or the courts determine that this has affected the fairness of the detention and the evidence obtained from it, under section 76 of the Police and Criminal Evidence Act 1984 (concerning oppression and circumstances rendering any admission unreliable during detention), and section 77 (concerning mentally vulnerable people where the evidence is based wholly or substantially on confession evidence), any admission in the interview can be dismissed.

The decision about whether to call the CPN, FME, or an interpreter is subject to the discretion of the custody officer. The custody officer has a duty to inform the detainee of their right to independent and free legal advice, and to allow the detainee to call their own solicitor, or a duty solicitor, accessed by the police from a list given to them. However the AA can call a solicitor on the detainee's behalf if they believe this is necessary (Home Office 2004: paragraph 3.19), and can suggest that one of the listed others be called, if required.

Palmer and Hart concluded from their research that custody officers often call an FME before calling an AA, but state that this is a misinterpretation of the Codes. Custody officers should call an AA at the same time, if the detainee 'appears to be' mentally disordered, and not just because they want them in on the interview when the custody officer or the FME or solicitor has requested an AA's attendance. Custody officers can also be confused about the difference in calling an Approved Social Worker for a Mental Health Act 1983 assessment, and calling an experienced mental health social worker as an AA (Bean and Nemitz, 1995).

The officer in the case is the officer who undertakes the interview, usually in a special interview room with a dedicated tape recorder that provides the definitive record of what happens and what is said in the interview. They are also bound by the Home Office 2004 Codes of Practice.

The police surgeon, or Forensic Medical Examiner (FME) as they are now usually known, is required to be called by the custody officer if it appears that a detainee 'appears to be suffering from a mental disorder' (Home Office, 2004: paragraph 9.5). There is no requirement for an FME to be called if someone appears to be learning disabled, though the term mental disorder under the MHA 1983 does include learning disabilities. In addition, medical attention should be called if a detainee appears to need it, or if a mental health assessment is needed under the MHA 1983.

However, most FMEs will be GPs, and have no particular expertise in mental health issues, and almost certainly none in learning disabilities. Palmer and Hart's research found that obtaining FMEs with such expertise was often problematic, and all those they interviewed had not received any initial training in the role. This is now changing, some police forces provide assistance and the Association of Forensic Physicians has guidance on the role and training of FMEs on their website, http://www.afpweb.org.uk/Pages/Publications-Education&Training.htm

Palmer and Hart also found that cases were often not pursued if they were minor offences, to save the police from all the procedures required for those from these vulnerable groups, but also, importantly, to not detain the person there longer than necessary. FMEs were often not called if the police had prior experience or knowledge of the detainee, and therefore were aware an AA was needed, and FME assessment was not necessary. However, as someone's mental heath problems may change, and remit, this may be a problem in number of situations.

Robertson's study of the role of the police surgeon (1992) found that most call-outs related to physical illness or injury. Only nine per cent of cases of requests for attendance related to mental illness, and only 0.5 per cent to 'mental handicap', as the study termed it.

One FME interviewed by Palmer and Hart stated that:

. . . even police officers do not understand what we are doing.

They found accord on the role of the FME in their part in determining fitness to be detained and interviewed, but not on their role in recommending an AA. In *R.* v. *Aspinall* (Times Law Report, 4 February 1999), the FME who examined the detainee determined that the latter was lucid at the time, and that he was fit to be interviewed, even though he was taking anti-psychotic drugs. After 13 hours in detention, he was asked if he wanted a solicitor or anyone else present, including an AA, but he said he wanted to go home, so refused. The Court of Appeal held that the subsequent interview took place in breach of the Home Office Codes, and was ruled inadmissible, as it had ignored the wide range of the AA's duties. There is no clear role for FMEs in ensuring an AA should be called, even if they determine fitness to be interviewed. In relation to fitness to be detained, the criteria for MHA 1983 assessment tend to be used, and assessments arranged if needed. In relation to fitness to be interviewed, Palmer and Hart found that this was a relatively recent addition to the FMEs' role. There was some confusion on whether they are assessing just physical fitness or mental fitness as well. Their role, whilst not changed, now needs to be viewed in relation to the Home Office's widened remit concerning who can assess and treat detainees for their health needs, under a new generic term of 'appropriate health care professional'.

The appropriate health care professional is a new role arising from the revised Codes of 2004. These are clinically qualified persons working within the scope of practice as determined by their relevant professional body. These may include FMEs, or nurses, for example. Such professionals will identify and quantify risks; inform the custody officer if the detainee's condition is likely to improve, or will require or be amenable to treatment; and indicate how long it may take for such improvement to take effect. These considerations and recommendations will be set out in writing as part of the custody record (Home Office 2004: paragraph 6, Annex G).

Community Psychiatric Nurses (CPNs) are now employed as Forensic Community Mental Health Nurses (FCMHNs) to provide services in police stations in certain parts of the country, such as in Warwickshire. They are available to provide advice and services to vulnerable groups in the police station, as often the FMEs are not specially qualified or experienced in mental health work. Their role is different from that of the Community Psychiatric Nurse who works outside the police station in the community, where they have a wider role that involves regular visits to people with mental health problems, usually in their own home. They may well be called on by the police to act as AAs, either as people who know the detainee or who have expertise in mental health work. They may now also may be called under the new role of 'appropriate health care professional'. For further discussion of the role of the Forensic Community Mental Health Nurse, see Phil Wood's Chapter 8 on diversion schemes.

Solicitors are bound by the law, and by the Rules and Codes of Practice of the Law Society, their professional body. Their role is to represent their client, protect their interests and uphold their legal rights, during the detention and the interview, and possibly later in court. They have the right to see their clients in private, and may advise their client of their right to silence, enabling them to give a 'no comment' interview while in detention. By law, communications between a solicitor and their client are subject to legal privilege; that is, the solicitor must not reveal to the police, or anyone else, any evidence or admission which the client has disclosed to them, and similarly, the client is entitled to keep to themselves any advice their lawyer has given them. This is not true of communications between other professionals and detainees. Almost all other professionals will, on the contrary, be *bound* to disclose to the police any admission which the detainee has made to them, either because their professional code of conduct requires it, or, because it is a requirement of their employing agency. It is important that such other professionals make clear to the detainee that whilst they are there to have regard to their welfare and rights, they do not need to know, indeed *should not know*, if the detainee thinks they have committed an offence.

The revised Home Office Codes in 1991 (and carried through into the most recent 2004 Codes) make it clear that a solicitor cannot act as AA when acting in a professional capacity as solicitor, emphasising the difference in roles. The solicitor is there solely to represent the legal interests of their client; the AA is there also to aid communication between the detainee and the police.

A further difference is that the solicitor can be barred by the police if they are causing problems in allowing the police to put questions properly to the detainee; there is no provision in the Codes for the police to bar an AA.

A psychiatrist may become involved if a detained person appears to be mentally disordered to the extent that they are unable to be interviewed. The Codes of Practice require the police to call a psychiatrist and an Approved Social Worker in such circumstances, to assess the detainee under the MHA 1983. This could lead to the detainee being detained against their will under the Act within the psychiatric system. This process may be implemented because the police recognise the need for this or because the AA or CPN attending recommends this, and the custody officer agrees.

The Approved Social Worker (ASW) is a qualified social worker who has undertaken additional specialist training in mental health issues and the application of the Mental Health Act 1983, and is provided by the local authority. Their task is to make independent assessments in conjunction with 'section 12' doctors, who assess whether the detainee has a mental disorder under the Mental Health Act 1983. A decision concerning whether the detainee may have to be detained involuntarily under the Act will then be made. The grounds for the ASW's assessment under section 13(2) of the Mental Health Act 1983 relate to whether the detention of the detainee is in all the circumstances of the case the most appropriate way of providing the care and medical treatment which they need. This may happen if the FME assesses the detainee to be in need of such an assessment, or if during detention an AA determines there is a high level of vulnerability that needs assessment, and the police agree to this. The ASW may well be called by the police to act as an AA, not in their ASW role, but as professionals who know the detainees and have expertise in mental health work. The ASW needs to clearly establish the remit for attendance at the police station, to ensure there is no conflict of interest for the detainee. It is inappropriate for the ASW to 'swap' roles, as this will be potentially confusing and possibly oppressive for the detainee.

An interpreter will be needed if the person cannot communicate in English, or has hearing or speech impairment. For people with learning disabilities, someone who can use Makaton or other facilitated communication systems may be required. It is the duty of the police to find the interpreter. The interpreter should be there just to interpret, and not act in any other role.

The Appropriate Adult role is described by John Pearse, a Unit Commander in the Metropolitan Police, and a long standing researcher in this field, as the most important contemporary safeguard for vulnerable suspects detained and interviewed by the police especially for those who are mentally disordered or learning disabled (Pearse, 2001).

The 'Appropriate Adult' role is set out in Code C of the Home Office (2004) Police and Criminal Evidence Act 1984 Codes of Practice. It states that:

'. . . [The appropriate adult] shall be informed that they are not expected to act simply as an observer; and the purpose of their presence is to advise the person being interviewed; observe whether the interview is being conducted properly and fairly; facilitate communication with the person being interviewed.*

(Code C, 2004, paragraph 11.17)

The AA role is separate and distinct from that of the solicitor; in addition to safeguarding the rights of the detainee, the AA has the additional role of facilitating communication with the police. Apart from this, there is little 'official' guidance for the AA on what they have powers to do, or on how they can carry out this role effectively. There is, though, a document entitled *Guidance for Appropriate Adults* on the Home Office website (www.homeoffice.gov.uk/docs/guidanceappadultscustody.pdf) which sets out some basic propositions; for example, that the AA has the right to call a solicitor on the detainee's behalf, even if the detainee has not exercised this right; and that the AA has an active role in protecting the detainees' rights. This may include not feeling that they have to remain silent during the interview if it is in the best interests of the detainee not to do so, and intervening in interviews in the interests of the detained person to help them communicate effectively with the police. This clarifies, as implied in the Codes, that the role is intended to be active rather than passive, and challenges what many custody officers may believe, that AAs are just there for 'welfare' reasons (Bean and Nemitz, 1995).

The current problems in appropriate adult provision

The potential for discrimination against mentally vulnerable people held for questioning is considerable. The following section sets out the problems for the police, AAs and detainees with the AA role.

The availability of AAs

The police often have difficulties in obtaining the attendance of an AA, and there are issues about who attends and how competent they are in fulfilling the role.

For mentally vulnerable adults, the police are required to try to obtain attendance of someone from the following list:
- A relative, guardian or other person responsible for their welfare.
- Someone experienced in dealing with mentally disordered or mentally vulnerable people but who is not a police officer or employed by the police.
- Failing these, some other responsible adult aged 18 or over who is not a police officer or employed by the police (Home Office, 2004; paragraph 1.7b).

Because the police are able to use relatives, or other adults not employed by the police in the AA role, there are variations across the country as to who is called as an Appropriate Adult, and therefore what service vulnerable adult detainees can expect to receive, and to what standard. The detainee may gain the services of an AA who is a professional from one of the statutory agencies such as social services, probation or health who may or may not be trained and knowledgeable in the role. The AA may be a volunteer from one of the growing number of Appropriate Adult schemes, or a relative. In desperation, it has been known for police officers to resort to a member of the public who happens to be passing the police station, people producing driving documents, a nearby hotel porter, the police station cleaner, or potentially, just about any one who happens to be nearby at the time (Pearse, 2001; Medford et al., 2000).

There are frequently difficulties for the police in procuring the attendance of an AA within a reasonable time frame (Palmer and Hart, 1996; Medford et al., 2000). One major problem resulting from such delays is the effect on the well-being and suggestibility of mentally vulnerable suspects who have to endure such prolonged periods of police detention, which is recognised as inherently coercive (Gudjonsson, 1992).

From a custody officer's perspective, they are often faced with a dilemma of detaining a person pending the arrival of an AA (to read their rights, undertake an interview or charge the person) or releasing them. This is one of the greatest weaknesses of the AA safeguard.

There is no specific duty on local authorities or health authorities to provide AAs for vulnerable adults, as there is for local authorities to provide AAs for juveniles. Often, AA provision is not a key focus for managers and policy makers in local authorities, and this area of provision falls into a gap between different managers' responsibilities. This is now further complicated by joint mental health and learning disabilities provision between local authority and health agencies, although this has had the effect in many areas of ensuring better provision, as nurses as well as social workers have been available to act in the AA role.

In the worst cases, detention can last for many hours before the arrival of the AA. Medford, Gudjonsson and Pearse (2000) found in their research concerning detained adults that 4.3 per cent of detainees were vulnerable in some way. Sixty per cent (N = 600) were not afforded the protection and support of an AA. The average wait for an AA to agree to attend for a vulnerable adult and then actually arrive was nearly six hours, but some had to wait for over 20 hours.

These delays create significant problems for the police and the detainee. Too often the detainee will wish to escape the stress of detention as quickly as possible, and this will add to the possibility of false confessions and unreliable evidence.

The suitability of AAs

Those who act as Appropriate Adults, both professionals and non-professionals, can frequently fail to carry out their role effectively, either through lack of knowledge and confidence, or because of the nature of the relationship with the detainee.

Robertson et al. carried out research in this area, stating that:

All three authors [of this research] *acted in the capacity of appropriate adult in interviews. Despite our professional backgrounds and our familiarity with police stations and police procedures, we all felt that we had little idea what was required of us or what we were allowed to do in terms of intervention. It is made clear to Appropriate Adults by the police that they are free to interject and object if they think this is necessary, but we imagine that very few people who act as appropriate adults know when it would be appropriate to object and that even fewer would have the courage to interrupt the police in their business of questioning someone.*

(Robertson et al., 1995)

There is clear evidence from available research that relatives have difficulty in providing a detached and independent service (Littlechild, 2001). Whilst most of this research relates to juveniles it is highly likely that this will hold true for relatives of vulnerable adult detainees, too. Gudjonsson (1993) has identified that parents are quite likely to resort to bullying tactics, and also that some relatives may suffer from a mental disorder or vulnerability to an extent similar to or even greater than the suspect's.

One of the authors of this chapter is aware of very experienced and qualified individuals who have performed the role of Appropriate Adult many times. However, when called upon to act as an Appropriate Adult for one their own relatives, they say that they are too emotionally involved and are unable to provide a professional and effective service.

If this is the case, then it can be argued that they are not suitable AAs. The main roles of the AA, as far as the criminal justice system is concerned, are to facilitate communication between the police and the detainee, and to have regard to the detainee's interests and welfare in a general sense, whilst they are detained in the police station. There is good reason to believe that relatives of vulnerable adults may also have difficulties not only in dealing with the emotions raised by having their relative detained, but also in understanding the nature of this role.

For example, in the case of *R. v. Morse and others* (Criminal Law Review 195, 1991), the judge found that an Appropriate Adult who is unable to discharge any or all the duties attributable to the role is an inappropriate choice and puts the interviewee at a disadvantage. In this case, the judge accepted psychiatric evidence that a father who had an IQ in the range 60–70 and was unable to read was not suitable to act as an AA for his 16-year-old son. The concerns about relatives intervening and their methods of doing so are highlighted in the case of *R. v. Jefferson* ([1994] All E.R. 270) where the AA was the father. Whilst he intervened on the side of the police, and often contradicted the young person's account, the young person's eventual confession of riot and violent behaviour was allowed to stand by the Court of Appeal. This was probably due to the fact the young person did not change his account of events as a result of his father's interventions; if he had done so, the courts may have found differently. This means that it is possible for such evidence to be admissible where this has happened, although other case law, e.g. in the case of *R.* v. *Morse and others* mentioned above, suggests the opposite.

In vulnerable adult cases, there is consistent evidence from research that indicates that the person called upon to act as an AA is unlikely to have any experience of the role, have little or no knowledge of the law, and is very unlikely to be familiar with or assertive enough to contend with the formal and intimidating regime inside a police station (Brown et al., 1992; Evans 1993a, 1993b; Robertson et al., 1995; Palmer and Hart, 1996). In instances where the carer or parent is not carrying out their role properly, a social worker or someone else from a social care or health agency or approved AA scheme (see Littlechild, 2001) should be called out instead, to ensure the role is carried out appropriately and with the proper training and support which they should have.

Effective appropriate adult practice

One key area identified from the interviews with consumers and providers of AA services as set out previously was the importance of the detainees' reassurance that the AA was attending to secure their well-being and rights. Vital aspects of the AA role, identified from research with people with vulnerabilities who have been detained and had AAs called on their behalf, are that the AA makes them feel confident they know what they are doing, that they explain the role to them, and are prepared to be proactive in this role, e.g. checking they understand the meaning of questions, and what is happening. It is also important that the AA makes clear their independence from the police; not only by telling them this, but also by making sure they do not appear over-friendly with the police, as the detainee may take this as a sign they should not trust them (Littlechild, 2001).

What follows are some brief checklists for AAs. For a full exposition of the role, see Littlechild (1996) for all the processes the professional attending may be involved in, e.g. reviews of detention at set time limits; strip and non-intimate and intimate body searches; taking intimate and non-intimate body samples; fingerprinting; photographing; identification procedures; charging, and complaints, amongst others. The checklists cover what to do on being requested to attend; what to do on arrival at the police station; and engaging with the detainee.

Actions to take when called as an appropriate adult

When requested to attend as an AA, there are a number of areas to explore with the police before agreeing to attend:

- The officer should be asked who else has been called? The AA should check if the 'knock-down' list for who should be called as an AA has been followed; see list in Code C, paragraph 1.17, set out previously on p26.
- Why have the other possible AAs, relatives or guardians, been ruled out?
- What are the details of apprehension; the nature of investigation, for what is the detainee held?
- Was there any force used in the detention?
- Have any checks been made with any other professionals who may know the person, to check as part of the assessment of the vulnerability of the detainee?

The police are often not well trained in recognising and dealing with people with mental health or learning disabilities, so it is useful to check why they think they need an AA: if it is because the detainee cannot read for example, this does not mean they are in need of an AA as defined by the Codes of Practice, unless they also have mental health or learning disabilities.

- How long is the detention likely to last? Most interviews will last less than an hour, but some can last considerably longer. It is important that the police know if the AA will have to leave by a certain time.
- Has a solicitor been called? If so, it is essential to ascertain when they are likely to arrive, so that arrival times can be co-ordinated; by speaking to the solicitor on their mobile phone if necessary, to minimise waiting times for all concerned.
- What is the alleged offence that is being investigated? If a solicitor has not been called, the AA may wish to call one at this stage, if they think the possible charge is serious enough, for example, as the AA can do this independently of the detainee (Code C, paragraph 3.19).
- For how long has the person been detained? Were they helping the police with inquiries voluntarily before being detained? This is important in relation to the 'custody clock' referred to in the next section.

On arrival at the police station

On arrival at the police station, check the custody record, and the risk assessment, which will have been completed by the custody officer, and include any assessments or recommendations from the appropriate health professional, if one was called. These are held by the custody officer. Check when the statement of rights which has to be given to detainees, was first given. It is good practice to keep notes of your discussions with the custody officer during the interview, whether taped or not.

It is important to ensure the detainee is again advised, even if told already, of their right to a free solicitor, at any time, and of their right to consult the Codes of Practice at any time. The AA must countersign a copy of a document saying this statement of rights has been read, and also ensure that the caution is given, which emphasises that they do not need to answer questions. There should be discussion with the solicitor about the AAs role and also with the detainee, separately from any police officers. This is to explain the AAs role, and which agency they are from. The AA can see the detainee on their own at any time during the detention (Code C, 3.18).

The detainee must be informed of their rights and the reason for the detention in the presence of the AA (Code C paragraph 3.17). This process will also form part of the AAs assessment, which will encompass spending a few minutes exploring general 'enquiry' questions, ascertaining the detainee's experience of the arrest and detention, before moving on to explain the AA role, and issues of confidentiality. The AA will then start to have an idea of the detainee's possible vulnerability, how worried they are, and how they are experiencing the detention. If after discussions with the officer, and after scrutinising the custody officer's risk assessment, the AA thinks they may be at risk of violence, the AA should see the detainee and have these discussions with an officer present, or nearby, when explaining their role.

If there are concerns about the vulnerability of the detainee, either before or during the interview, the AA can ask to see them on their own to check how they are experiencing the questioning and how they are reacting. The AA can make representations to the interviewing officer to say that they think the person does not understand the situation, the questions, and the answers they are giving. The police can still determine to continue if they wish, though this could be used in evidence later if the matter goes to court. The AA will need to assess whether it is best to say this to the officer on their own or in the presence of the detainee, and whether to ask for a further assessment by the FME or appropriate health professional.

The AA should at all times be aware of the rights of the detainee, and bring these to the attention of the interviewing and/or custody officer if they believe they are not being kept to: they have rights to medical help, and eight hours sleep (normally at night); to be interviewed in a room that is adequately lit, ventilated and heated; to know who the interviewing officer is; and to have meal and refreshment breaks. For details of these provisions, see Code C, section 8.

If the AA objects to any aspect of the detention or the police's interviewing procedures at any time, they should ask for this to be recorded on the custody record, a copy of which AAs now (from the 1991 Codes on) have a right to receive. The custody officer must investigate any such complaint (Home Office, 2004: paragraph 9.2).

Keep aware of the 'custody clock' under sections 40(2) and (3) the Police and Criminal Evidence Act 1984, when reviews of the necessity for the continued detention should take place. The detainee may not be kept longer than 24 hours – depending when the 'custody clock' starts to run – without being charged, unless a superintendent or more senior officer agrees to the maximum limit of 36 hours.

Engaging with the detainee

It is important that the AA informs the detainee that there is no confidentiality agreement within this AA role, so it is best they do not tell the AA about the alleged offence, as they may have to inform the police. The AA should ensure the detainee knows the AA is there to ensure the detainee's welfare, and to check if questions are appropriate to their mental state and level of understanding. The AA should inform the detainee of the right to consult in private, and to call a solicitor on their behalf if they believe this is necessary.

A further area to be considered is whether the detainee is fit to be interviewed. The FME may not be expert in mental health or learning disabilities. It may be necessary to check if another suitable appropriate health professional has been called, and what their assessments and recommendations are. The AA's private interview is also part of an assessment of this, as is whether they need an interpreter.

In the interview, the AA can intervene to ensure the detainee understands the questions put or line of questioning, and to help them clarify an answer if this seems unclear.

The AA needs to be aware of the ongoing right to a solicitor; if they think the detainee needs one, they can stop the interview and call a solicitor on behalf of the detainee.

Conclusion

This chapter has examined the roles of those who may be involved in dealing with people with mental disorder and mental vulnerabilities when they are detained by police as the result of their suspected involvement in an offence. In particular the role of the AA has been appraised. The importance of acting confidently and effectively in the role of AA has been considered, as has how this might be achieved, to protect the rights and interests of detainees from the vulnerable groups designated under the Home Office Codes of Practice 2004.

References

Bean, P. and Nemitz, T. (1995) *Out of Depth and Out of Sight*, London: Mencap.

Brown, D., Ellis, T. and Larcombe, K. (1992) *Changing the Code: Police Detention Under the Revised PACE Codes of Practice.* Home Office Research Study 129. London: HMSO.

Clare, I. and Gudjonsson, G. (1992) *Devising and Piloting an Experimental Version of the Notice to Detained Persons.* Research Study No. 7. London: The Royal Commission on Criminal Justice/HMSO.

Evans, R. (1993a) *The Conduct of Police Interviews with Juveniles.* Research Study No. 8. London: The Royal Commission on Criminal Justice/HMSO.

Evans, R. (1993b) Getting things taped. *Community Care.* Nov. 19.

Fearns, D. (2001a) Learning disabilities: one person's use. In Littlechild, B. (Ed.) *Appropriate Adults and Appropriate Adult Schemes: Service User, Provider and Police Perspectives.* Birmingham: Venture Press.

Fearns, D. (2001b) Learning disabilities: recognition and risk. In Littlechild, B. (Ed.) *Appropriate Adults and Appropriate Adult Schemes: Service User, Provider and Police Perspectives.* Birmingham: Venture Press.

Gudjonsson, G.H. (1992) *The Psychology of Interrogations, Confessions and Testimony.* Chichester: John Wiley.

Gudjonsson, G.H. (1993) Confession Evidence, Psychological Vulnerability and Expert Testimony. *Journal of Community and Applied Social Psychology.* 3: 117–29.

Gudjonsson, G.H., Clare, I.C., Rutter, S. and Pearse, J. (1993) *Persons at Risk During Interviews in Police Custody: The Identification of Vulnerabilities.* Research Study No. 12. London: The Royal Commission on Criminal Justice/Home Office Research and Planning Unit.

Hansen, G. (2001a) Mental heath problems: one person's use. In Littlechild, B. (Ed.) *Appropriate Adults and Appropriate Adult Schemes: Service User, Provider and Police Perspectives.* Birmingham: Venture Press.

Hansen, G. (2001b) Mental heath problems: recognition and risk. In Littlechild, B. (Ed.) *Appropriate Adults and Appropriate Adult Schemes: Service User, Provider and Police Perspectives.* Birmingham: Venture Press.

Home Office (2004) *The Police and Criminal Evidence Act 1984:* Code of Practice C. Revised edn. London: The Stationery Office.

Littlechild, B. (1996) *The Police and Criminal Evidence Act 1984: The Role of the Appropriate Adult.* Birmingham: British Association of Social Workers.

Littlechild, B. (Ed.) (2001) *Appropriate Adults and Appropriate Adult Schemes: Service User, Provider and Police Perspectives.* Birmingham: Venture Press.

Medford, S., Gudjonsson, G.H. and Pearse, J. (2000) *The Identification of Persons at Risk in Police Custody: The Use of Appropriate Adults by the Metropolitan Police.* Metropolitan Police.

Observer, The (2003) *Soham Police Force Face Clampdown on Data.* The Observer. 21 Dec.

Palmer, C. and Hart, M. (1996) *A PACE in the Right Direction?* Institute for the Study of the Legal Profession, University of Sheffield.

Pearse, J. (1995) Police interviewing: the identification of vulnerabilities. *Journal of Community and Applied Social Psychology.* 5: 147–59.

Pearse, J. (2001) The problems associated with implementing the appropriate adult safeguard. In Littlechild, B. (Ed.) *Appropriate Adults and Appropriate Adult Schemes: Service User, Provider and Police Perspectives.* Birmingham: Venture Press.

Pearse, J. and Gudjonsson, G.H. (1996) Understanding the problems of the appropriate adult. *Expert Evidence.* 4: 3, 101–4.

Pearse, J. and Gudjonsson, G.H. (1996) How appropriate are appropriate adults? *Journal of Forensic Psychiatry.* 7: 3, 570–80.

Pearse, J. and Gudjonsson, G.H. (1999) Measuring influential police interviewing tactics: a factor analysis approach. *Legal and Criminological Psychology.* 4: 221–38.

Robertson, G. (1992) *The Role of the Police Surgeon.* Research Study No. 6. London: The Royal Commission on Criminal Justice/Home Office Research and Planning Unit.

Robertson, G., Pearson, R. and Gibb, R. (1995) *The Entry of Mentally Disordered People to the Criminal Justice System.* Research Findings No. 21. London: Home Office Research and Statistics Department.

Chapter 3

Mentally Vulnerable Victims and Witnesses

Sally Angus

Introduction

This chapter examines the experiences of victims within the criminal justice system, and particularly the special features appropriate to, and as they may be experienced by, adults with mental health problems or learning disabilities.

Figures from the 2002/03 British Crime Survey revealed there were just under 5.9 million crimes in England and Wales reported to the police (Simmons and Dodd, 2003).

So how do victims cope with having been burgled, robbed or assaulted? How does society respond to victims? Do we stereotype victims like we do offenders? Are we more sympathetic towards some victims than others? It can be argued that the answer to the last two questions is 'yes', and that the media to some extent exacerbates our stereotypes. Consider the following headings:

Elderly pensioner robbed of life savings outside post office.

and

Youths on rampage outside takeaway.

Where are our sympathies drawn? The first headline clearly identifies the victim, and our reactions and responses are ones of horror and abhorrence. An *innocent* victim. The second headline conjures up thoughts of young people, probably male, probably drunk, causing mayhem in an otherwise peaceful town centre. It certainly does not conjure up thoughts of victims, let alone *innocent* victims!

Both these headlines appeared in my local newspaper in the same week, back in the early 1990s, when I managed a Victim Support Scheme in North London.

Whilst the first heading (which incidentally appeared on the front page) clearly identifies the victim, the latter does not. Further exploration results in the discovery of four young male victims caught up in this incident. They had left a club earlier that evening and were in a takeaway food outlet, when a fight broke out. They were not drunk, they did not instigate the fight, but all four suffered serious injuries. So what are the implications for a society where we determine the legitimacy of victims by age, gender, race or any other difference? My experiences of working with young male victims of crime is that they are not recognised as victims and consequently find it very difficult for their victimisation to be acknowledged and to receive help. They are just one example of certain groups within society whose experiences of crime are compounded by society's assumptions.

Another example of such a group is people with mental illness. A recent report in *The Guardian* newspaper revealed that people with severe mental illness, living in the community, are more than twice as likely to be victims of violence as the general public, and are less likely to report such incidents (*The Guardian*, 2003)

People with learning disabilities are another group disadvantaged by the criminal justice system and society's attitudes towards them. Mencap (1999) published a report called *Living in Fear*, which highlighted that 75 per cent of people with a learning disability report instances of crime or harassment after they have happened, but only 17 per cent report such incidents directly to the police. Williams (1995) found that the police rarely become involved in incidents involving people with learning disabilities.

How victims cope in the aftermath of crime is determined to some extent by their own coping mechanisms and the response of others, such as family and friends, and those within the criminal justice system. The next few pages of this chapter will explore the social construction of victimisation and look at the impact of crime upon victims and their needs in the aftermath of the crime.

Government response to victims

Successive governments have attempted to use victims' issues to support law and order campaigns. Brian Williams makes reference to the small proportion of the criminal justice budget allocated to victim assistance, despite political rhetoric purportedly prioritising victims:

> *Victims' needs have been the subject of lip-service, but have not received the degree of attention devoted to offenders.*

> (Williams, 1999)

However, the victim movement in the UK has slowly but surely influenced policy, re-instituting the victim as a key participant in the criminal justice system. This movement continues to see the inexorable replacement of 'needs' with 'rights'. Clearly there has been significant political interest in the plight of victims.

This renewed interest in victims in recent years has led to a number of initiatives and changes in legislation providing an enhanced voice for victims. The introduction of *The Victims Charter* in 1990 was an early indication of a change in government thinking regarding victims, giving them a more central role in the criminal justice process.

The revised *Victims Charter* of 1996 (Home Office, 1996) is referred to as 'a statement of service standards for victims of crime' and sets out a number of 'expectations' victims and witnesses should have of the criminal justice system and the service delivered by agencies within it.

The Charter sets out a number of expectations for victims:

You can expect:

- *A crime you have reported to be investigated and to receive information about what happens.*
- *The chance to explain how the crime has affected you and your interests to be taken into account.*
- *To be treated with respect and sensitivity, if you have to go to court as a witness.*
- *To be offered emotional and practical support.*

(Home Office, 1996)

The Charter also provides guidance and advice if victims or witnesses wish to make a complaint against any of the agencies within the criminal justice system.

What is less clear is the rationale behind Home Office initiatives that recognise and have the appearance of acceding to victims' demands.

Two incentives may have conspired to increase the state's involvement with victim issues:

- Firstly, placating victims is a political manoeuvre designed to divert attention away from successive governments' failure to reduce the incidence of crime (Williams, 1999).
- Secondly, the government has realised the importance of victims and witnesses engaging with the criminal justice process and their crucial role in bringing offenders to justice; during 2001 over 30,000 cases were abandoned because victims and witnesses either failed to attend court or refused to give evidence (Home Office, 2002a: 36).

So what is available to victims? The largest agency delivering a service to victims in the United Kingdom is Victim Support, a national, independent, voluntary organisation providing practical help and emotional support to victims of crime. Victim Support, currently receiving a grant of approximately two per cent of the criminal justice budget, is the only voluntary sector organisation providing a service within the criminal justice system. It is the fastest growing charity of the last decade and, in 2002, had provided a service to over one million victims and witnesses (Victim Support, 2002). In addition to Victim Support there are a number of smaller agencies, such as Women's Aid and Rape Crisis, offering support to victims and survivors of specific crimes. Victim Support continues to lobby on behalf of victims, a role it has pursued with considerable success in recent years. In 1995 Victim Support published *The Rights of Victims of Crime* (Victim Support, 1995: 15). Whilst these rights were not enshrined in legislation, they acted as a catalyst for change. Since 1995 there have been a number of initiatives, some statutory, and some not, which have increasingly provided a voice for victims. For example, the Protection from Harassment Act 1997 now protects victims and witnesses reporting crimes from possible reprisals from the defendant. The introduction of Victim Personal Statements in 2001 provides the victim with an opportunity to:

> . . . *tell the criminal justice agencies and services dealing with their care, how the crime has affected them.*

(Home Office, 2001a)

The same year saw the introduction of the Criminal Justice and Court Services Act 2000. Within the legislation there is a requirement for the National Probation Service to contact victims who have suffered a sexual or violent crime, for which the offender received a custodial sentence of one year or more. The National Probation Service is now required to make contact with the victim within two months of the sentence with the intention of providing the victim with information about the sentence. They are required to ask the victim if they wish for any further contact from the Probation Service and establish whether the victim wants the service to contact them when the prisoner is due for release.

This recognition of fear is particularly important for victims with mental health problems, who may have particular concerns and apprehension, due to their experiences of discrimination and poor attitudes towards people with such problems. This may be particularly true for people who may have paranoid feelings, or are depressed, for example. The sense of isolation can be overwhelming and can mean that the victim 'personalises' the crime, adding to their feelings of paranoia or deepening the level of depression. For those with learning disabilities, the issues are often more complex. Often, particularly where a sexual offence or violence has been committed, the victim usually knows the perpetrator, so the issue of fear may be greater. It is known that people with learning disabilities are at a greater risk of having crimes committed against them when compared with the general population (Wilson and Brewer, 1992; Brown et al., 1995; Williams, 1995; Mencap, 2001). Equally, people with learning disabilities are less likely to receive justice through the courts, therefore may live in fear of the perpetrator for a significant period of time. They are also likely to find that the crime committed against them will not be considered seriously by the police, will not be recorded as crime, nor will it be prosecuted by the Crown Prosecution Service (CPS). Even if a case is successfully prosecuted, a victim with a learning disability will probably not receive the same follow-up as a person without a learning disability, and they may find that Victim Support is not in a position to offer appropriate support to them.

Nonetheless, in terms of engaging victims in the criminal justice process, the Crime and Disorder Act 1998 and the Youth Justice and Criminal Evidence Act 1999 have the greatest potential, being underpinned by restorative justice principles. This is the first time the theory of restorative justice has found its way into English legislation.

Whilst there are a number of definitions applied to restorative justice, Marshall provides a succinct version:

Restorative Justice is a process whereby the parties with a stake in a particular offence come together to resolve collectively how to deal with the aftermath of the offence and its implications for the future.

(Marshall, 1999)

The underlying ethos is that victims should have the opportunity to say how the crime has affected them and along with representatives of the community, confront offenders with the impact of their crimes, and ensure they make reparation to victims. Currently restorative justice interventions are the preserve of the youth justice legislation, although the government has produced a consultative document on its strategy to introduce restorative justice initiatives into work with adults (Home Office, 2003a).

Whilst research from the pilots of the Youth Offending Teams and Youth Offending Panels shows little victim participation (Holdaway et al., 2001; Newburn et al., 2001) it is important to acknowledge that the very fact that victims are asked to engage in restorative justice initiatives can be restorative. Up to now victims have not been offered that choice.

More recently the government has unveiled a 'National Strategy' to deliver improved services to victims and witnesses (Home Office, 2003b). The government wants to assure the public that they will do 'everything they can to make sure victims and witnesses are treated with respect' (2003b: 1).

In pursuit of this strategy, the government recently introduced the Domestic Violence, Crime and Victims Bill (2004) which seeks to place on a statutory footing a number of measures highlighted in an earlier government White Paper *Justice for All* (Home Office, 2002b). The measures include:

- Putting the existing Victims Advisory Panel on a statutory footing.
- Introducing a Code of Practice for victims, binding on all criminal justice agencies.

- Stronger legal protection for victims, by extending the use of restraining orders.
- Amendments to the Protection from Harassment Act 1997, ensuring victims have a voice with regard to any application to a change to a restraining order.
- Making the breaching of a non-molestation order a criminal offence.
- Making the causing or allowing of the death of a child or vulnerable adult a criminal offence.

An accompanying Code of Practice for victims will replace the existing *Victims Charter* (Home Office, 1996) and, whilst failures to adhere to the Code of Practice will not be actionable in either criminal or civil proceedings, the Code will be admissible in evidence in civil or criminal proceedings '. . . a court may take into account a failure to comply with the Code in determining a question in the proceedings' (section 15 (2)).

Redress for breaches of the Code will be via a complaints regime with the Parliamentary Commissioner for Administration being the final arbiter.

The Code widens its remit in terms of vulnerable victims and includes a victim who:

- Is under the age of 17 years.
- Is suffering from mental disorder (within the meaning of the Mental Health Act 1983).
- Has experienced domestic violence.
- Has been the subject of recorded or reported incidents of harassment or bullying.
- Has a history of self-neglect or self-harm.
- Has made an allegation of criminal conduct which constitutes a sexual offence or which is racially aggravated, or aggravated on religious, homophobic or transphobic grounds.
- Is the family spokesperson of a person who has died.
- Is likely to be or who has been subjected to intimidation in respect of the allegation of criminal conduct which the person has made.

However, the framework provided in the Youth Justice and Criminal Evidence Act 1999 will not be effective unless the various agencies work together to ensure the necessary support structures are in place to support people with mental health or learning disabilities, both individually and collectively, to improve services. Restorative justice is a particularly challenging concept for people with learning disabilities, as it requires a degree of confidence and self-esteem to be able to participate in the criminal justice system as an equal, and as stated earlier, it would appear that few victims of crime take up the opportunity to engage with the perpetrator. Clare and Murphy (2001) also acknowledge that:

. . . people with learning disabilities themselves need to be empowered to recognise, and respond to, crimes and other types of anti-social behaviour against themselves or others.

These same issues may also apply to people who have mental health problems, so agencies need to increase their awareness of the effects that crime may have on these vulnerable groups.

Vulnerable and intimidated victims and witnesses

As mentioned earlier in the chapter, we know the government is eager to engage victims and witnesses in the criminal justice process, in order to 'narrow the justice gap'. In this aptly named document *Narrowing the Justice Gap* (Home Office, 2002c), the Home Office identified the gap between the number of crimes recorded and the number which result in the offender being brought to justice. Many of the victims and witnesses are vulnerable and intimidated. Some ten per cent of crimes reported to the police result in witnesses being intimidated and at least 20 per cent of crimes are not reported to the police for fear of reprisals (Home Office, 2002c).

Elliot (1998) points out that several studies suggest that a large proportion of sexual crimes against people with intellectual disabilities are unreported to the police (see Sanders et al., 1996).

It seems plausible that this also applies to property offences, and to some people with physical disabilities or mental illness. Mencap (1999) found that 88 per cent of people with learning disabilities had experienced bullying in a one-year period, and that 53 per cent of the bullying continued, even after it had been reported. The majority of these incidents will not have been reported to the police, but even if they had been, it is doubtful if or what action would have been taken by the police.

The government White Paper *Speaking up for Justice* (Home Office, 1998) made 78 recommendations in relation to vulnerable and intimidated witnesses, some of which became enshrined in the Youth Justice and Criminal Evidence Act 1999. Recommendations not requiring new legislation have resulted in new policy, administrative action and training (Home Office, 2002a).

The Youth Justice and Criminal Evidence Act 1999 defines vulnerable witnesses as:
- Witnesses under the age of 17 years at the time of the hearing (s16.(1)(a)).
- Witnesses suffering from a mental disorder within the meaning of the Mental Health Act 1983 (s16.(2)(a)(i)).
- Witnesses that have a significant impairment of intelligence and social function (s16.(2)(2)(a)(ii)).
- Witnesses having a physical disability or suffering from a physical disorder (s16.(2)(b)).

Intimidated witnesses are defined as:
- Witness is likely to be diminished by reason of fear or distress in connection with testifying in the proceedings (s17.(1)).

Those witnesses defined as vulnerable or intimidated are then eligible for a number of 'special measures' that are not automatic, but are determined by the courts. Although the legislation now exists to provide victims and witnesses with a number of 'special measures' to help them provide 'best evidence', many are not yet in place and a number of pilot sites have been identified to evaluate the measures prior to implementation. The time scale for some important special measures is not yet clear and there is no guarantee that the Secretary of State will implement them. If, or when, a crime is reported and prosecuted, the victim who has a mental health problem or learning disability will need additional support above and beyond that which might ordinarily be expected. Home Office guidance for criminal justice professionals has been provided in the form of *Achieving Best Evidence in Criminal Proceedings: Guidance for Vulnerable or Intimidated Witnesses, including Children* (Home Office, 2002a) which provides detailed best practice guidance for both those special measures already implemented and those awaiting implementation following evaluation of the pilot trials.

The government in their recently published strategy for victims and witnesses has suggested the idea of 'Community Justice Centres'. Such centres would cater for children and vulnerable or intimidated witnesses, offering a supportive and safe environment to give evidence (Home Office 2003b: 24).

However defining 'vulnerable' and 'intimidated' is not straightforward. One could argue, that by the mere fact someone has become a victim, they are deemed vulnerable. Certainly children fall into the category of vulnerable by definition of age; but how do we determine adult vulnerability including those with mental health problems or those who have learning disabilities? The specific issue around mental illness was raised in a consultative paper published by the Scottish Executive. Concerns about defining and diagnosing mental illness in relation to vulnerability are complex and the following quote from the report succinctly sums up the problem:

> *Existence of a Court Order may not be a reliable guide to vulnerability. A person who has an insight into their illness and the effect it has on him, may be more fearful and distressed at the prospect of a court appearance than someone who does not believe he is ill and had to be given treatment compulsorily.*
>
> (Scottish Executive, 2002: 12)

The report goes on to say that the strict criteria set down within the legislation drastically limits the number of people with mental illnesses qualifying for special measures.

Impact of crime

The impact of crime upon the victim is complex and whilst there is not sufficient opportunity here to explore this in depth, it is important to consider some of the main issues. In the very early research on the establishment of the first Victim Support Scheme in Bristol in the early 1970s, it was discovered that the emotional impact of the crime upon the victim was more important to the victim than financial loss or physical pain (Maguire and Corbett, 1987).

The severity of the crime does not determine the impact upon the victim; people's responses are individual and therefore unpredictable (Williams, 1999). However, the experience of a victim of crime is different to that of someone who suffers an accident or an illness in that it involves an intentional act inflicted by one person on another. The unique nature of such intrusion is likely to have a profound effect on how crime victims perceive others (Reeves and Mulley, 2000: 126).

In the aftermath of crime victims can present with physical, psychological, emotional and behavioural symptoms. Apart from obvious physical injuries sustained during a violent crime, victims may suffer from a range of physical effects including, headaches, nausea, insomnia and lethargy (Victim Support, 1998). The psychological impact often presents in the victim feeling disempowered and with low self-esteem. The emotional impact of crime results in an array of responses such as shock, disbelief, fear, anger, guilt, self-blame and revenge. These are normal responses to an abnormal situation (Victim Support, 1998).

Behavioural change can also manifest itself in the victims using avoidance tactics to reduce the risk of the crime happening again. Such actions may include avoiding areas and situations that remind them of the crime; moving home, withdrawing from social contact or attempting to alter their appearance or behaviour (Victim Support, 1998). Research shows that long-term problems may arise if the victim is unable to resolve these emotional responses. Maguire and Bennett found that 65 per cent of burglary victims interviewed were still affected by the crime four to ten weeks after the burglary (cited in Williams, 1999: 53). The process of recovery is not dissimilar from bereavement. Victim Support has accumulated vast experience of working with the victim in dealing with the impact of crime. The model in Figure 1 is one that many Victim Support Schemes use in identifying the needs of crime victims.

The model is a four-stage process with the initial response of shock and denial giving way to a period of disorganisation or depression. Here the victims' feelings of self-blame may well result in low self-esteem again, a particular problem for a number of people with mental health problems and learning disabilities. Typically, the victim will then move through a stage of reconstruction and acceptance, acknowledging the crime and realising they

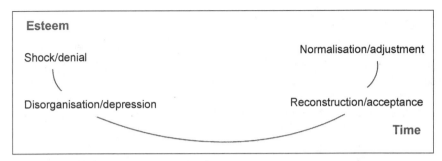

Figure 1 Process of recovery from violent crime

cannot 'turn the clock back', to a final stage of readjustment where the victim moves on (Victim Support, 1998). This is not life returning to 'normal', but a return of self-esteem and self-worth and a more positive view of the future. Whilst this model appears simplistic the time frame and process is individual to the victim and to a large extent may be determined by external factors such as the criminal justice system. Lengthy criminal justice processes – the resolution of the criminal trial and criminal injuries compensation claims – may compromise victims' ability to achieve early resolution and recovery. A plethora of factors are likely to affect victims' recovery. These might be external – the nature of the crime, and their innate resilience. Life stresses also affect victims' resilience and recovery; research shows that victims who have recently suffered a major stress such as bereavement, divorce, and job loss are more likely to be affected (Friedman and Tucker, 1997). If the victim has been a victim previously, there is evidence to suggest that a more complicated recovery process is likely. This is an important point as research shows that four per cent of victims suffer 41 per cent of all crime (Farrell and Pease, 1993) and being a victim of crime is 'the strongest single predictor of future victimisation' (Pease, 1998: 34). Access to social support is an important factor. If a victim has a supportive and understanding network of family and friends this will be a major positive influence on their ability to recover.

Finally a person's ability to recover from a crime is considerably improved when others recognise the significance of the event (Victim Support, 2002: 4). Sadly this is not always the norm and many victims experience secondary victimisation. This exists at both an individual and institutional level; a friend or family member who makes insensitive remarks or who in some way blames the victim; institutions that come into contact with the victim that fail to acknowledge the victim's experience. For people with mental health problems or learning disabilities, additional problems can arise if professionals who should be supporting them do not acknowledge the effects of victimisation, to support them positively through it.

Needs of victims

Information

Without doubt this is the most common concern raised by victims. Often victims know very little about the criminal justice process and they simply want to know what will happen and when. A pilot project set up to assist the victim in seeking information through a 'One Stop Shop' proved somewhat unsuccessful as much of the information victims wanted was in fact unavailable to them (Hoyle et al., 1999). For those witnesses attending court, such information is especially important. The court can seem a daunting and frightening place and being able to provide knowledge about the workings of the court is essential when supporting victims and witnesses. Victim Support already provides a comprehensive support programme in both the crown court and the Magistrates' court. Many of the recommendations made in 'Achieving Best Evidence' for the 'Court Witness Supporter' already exists through the delivery of service by Victim Support Witness Service volunteers (Home Office, 2002a: 147).

Recognition

Acknowledging the person's experiences of crime is important, an area often overlooked by criminal justice agencies (Victim Support, 1999). Recognition, particularly by those in authority, is important and a good understanding of the victim perspective should be a prerequisite for all those working within the criminal justice system. Part of the process of recognition is actually listening to victims and enabling them to tell their story. Often the constraints of the criminal justice system prevent victims from sharing their experiences. For example the role of the police is to investigate the crime and to this end officers need detailed information. The process of obtaining the relevant information from a victim creates an environment where victims are not necessarily encouraged to say how they feel. In court, victims have little opportunity to express their feelings as they are prevented from responding in any other way than by answering questions posed by counsel. It is only in recent years that prosecution counsel has actually acknowledged victims before giving evidence.

Part of the recognition process is about identifying witnesses who are particularly vulnerable. Research shows that mental health service users who have been victims of crime experience a very negative response from criminal justice agencies. They have difficulty in accessing criminal justice agencies and are often viewed as unreliable witnesses (McCabe and Ford, 2001: 7).

Similar experiences are common for people with learning disabilities. Extensive research (Williams, 1995; Clare and Gudjonsson, 1993; Sanders et al., 1996; Mencap, 2001) outlines the issues and difficulties faced by people with learning disabilities trying to access the criminal justice system. The primary issue centres on whether a person with a learning disability will be a 'reliable' witness, whether as a victim or a perpetrator of crime.

Respect

In an offender-driven criminal justice system, victims may not be treated with respect. Previous research shows that in some cases victims have been used to rehabilitate the offender rather than assist in their own recovery (Robinson, 1996). Respect is more than mere recognition. It requires a genuine commitment to both understand and meet the needs of victims, including awareness about diversity.

Safety

Victims of crime want to know that if they report the incident to the police they will not be intimidated by offenders or their supporters; and if that is the case, they will be taken seriously by the police. Services provided in the crown court by the Witness Service provide facilities to allow victims and witnesses to sit away from the main court area and therefore reduce the likelihood of meeting the defendant. A number of the 'special measures' rendered available by the Youth Justice and Criminal Evidence Act 1999, will reassure victims and witnesses about their safety and may reduce intimidation within the courtroom. The ability to give evidence via a televised link, rather than going into the courtroom or through the use of screens in the courtroom are just two measures that will assist. Other special measures, such as pre-recorded cross-examination and use of intermediaries, will possibly become available in due course.

Satisfaction

This is not about revenge, but about keeping promises or commitments to victims. Keeping them informed is enabling the victim to move on through the process of recovery. Satisfaction is also about getting access to appropriate services, compensation or information.

The future for victims of crime

Whilst there have been significant improvements for victims of crime in recent years, and we must not lose sight of that, nevertheless further changes are needed to enable victims to fully engage in the criminal justice process. Some changes have begun to have an impact and examples of good practice can be found. The Sandwell Vulnerable Witness Project is a case in point. The service is currently being piloted by Victim Support in Sandwell, in the West Midlands, and has achieved encouraging results. Since July 2001 the project has dealt with over 120 cases of victims and witnesses who referring agencies defined as 'vulnerable'. Key agencies such as the police, Crown Prosecution Service and the courts have referred people onto the project and the majority of the 120 referrals have resulted in successful convictions, suggesting that the support provided enabled witnesses to give their best possible evidence (Victim Support, 2003).

The government White Paper *Justice for All* recommended a programme of reform, guided by a single clear priority:

To rebalance the criminal justice system in favour of the victim and the community so as to reduce crime and bring more offenders to justice.

(Home Office, 2002b)

As mentioned earlier in this chapter, a number of recommendations made in the White Paper are currently subject to the Domestic Violence, Crime and Victims Bill 2004. However, the White Paper also identified the need to extend an understanding of the needs of victims beyond the courtroom into other government departments such as health and housing. Victim Support identified this failing in their publication *Criminal Neglect: No Justice Beyond Criminal Justice* (Victim Support, 2002). In this report Victim Support acknowledges efforts to meet victims' needs within the criminal justice system, but argues for a more holistic approach. The impact of crime permeates beyond the criminal justice system into many other areas, requiring services such as health, housing, education, insurance and social services to adopt policies and procedures that respond to their needs. The report makes the point that victims' needs should not be determined by either the crime suffered or by the profile of an offender; indeed 96 per cent of crime victims' cases remain undetected and do not proceed through the criminal justice system.

The White Paper suggests that victims should be at the heart of the criminal justice system and a number of initiatives are recommended including establishing a Victims Commissioner, supported by a National Victims Advisory Panel. Victim Support argues that crime affects the whole person and that victims' health and quality of life can suffer. These effects can be magnified where the victim has mental health problems or learning disabilities. Often the impact of crime ripples through people's lives and can be more devastating than the initial crime. If this is ignored, it can lead to a greater feeling of helplessness, despair and increase the feelings of powerlessness. The long-term effects may lead to unemployment, stigma, homelessness and a reliance on a few people for contact with the outside world. The *Valuing*

People strategy (DoH, 2001) also points out that people with learning disabilities are generally socially isolated, and only 30 per cent have a non-disabled friend, with only just fewer than 10 per cent being in any form of paid employment. This wide ranging impact of crime means that a whole array of services such as health, housing, education, insurance and social services need policies and procedures in place which recognise the needs of victims. They add that the wide range of needs should not be determined by either the nature of the crime suffered or by the type of offender. They point out that 96 per cent of victims of crime are those where the offenders are not detected and whose cases do not proceed through the criminal justice system. These are still victims of crime, experiencing the impact of crime, but currently do not have a voice.

Williams (1995) concludes that:

. . . redressing the stereotyped view of people with learning difficulties, in relation to crime, is the key element in changing the present situation. Justice is frustrated not only because of the response of the separate agencies, but of the effect they have on each other. The police do not record crimes because they believe the CPS will not prosecute, staff do not report to the police because they 'do nothing' and victims do not tell staff because they say 'the police won't help'.

Consequently the courts are unpractised at dealing with vulnerable witnesses, and perpetrators see people with learning disabilities as safe targets.

Unfortunately, the new Domestic Violence, Crime and Victims Bill 2004 does not address victims' needs outside of the criminal justice system.

In recent years Victim Support, whilst continuing to offer a support service to victims of crime, have also taken on a campaigning role on behalf of victims. The organisation has been instrumental in many legislative changes within the criminal justice system. However, a recent National Audit Office report has recommended that the Home Office review the delivery of support services to victims and witnesses (Audit Commission, 2002). This is likely to result in competitive tendering for such services following piloting of devolved court-based witness services.

Libby Purves suggests:

Under the new regime a benevolent, well-evolved pool of expertise, conditioned and accustomed to bat for the baffled individual, would be subordinated to the control of the statutory, professional criminal justice establishment.

(The Times, 2003)

Let us wait and see.

Case study 1

Mrs B is a 38-year-old Bangladeshi woman who was referred to Victim Support. Mrs B was a victim of criminal damage and common assault. Mr and Mrs B and their four children live on a high crime estate in North London. Mr B was a voluntary patient at a local psychiatric unit and had recently returned home. Mr and Mrs B believe the crime was racially motivated. The family had been subjected to on-going abuse by several white youths living on the estate. In this particular instance graffiti appeared on their garden fence and when Mrs B went out to remonstrate with the young male she believed responsible, she was spat at and verbally abused.

The family was living in fear; the children were frightened to leave their home to walk to school. Mr B was very anxious and the on-going incidents appeared to exacerbate his existing illness.

The police referred the family to Victim Support. A volunteer was assigned and worked with the family, supporting them through the process of a court case. Further support included liaison with the housing department and with the schools regarding the children's disrupted education. The volunteer, at the request of Mr and Mrs B, met with the CPN to discuss the court case and issues arising from it. The support was over a period of four months, followed by a clear understanding that the family could self-refer to the scheme if they required further support.

Case study 2

Mr N is a 43-year-old white male living in supported accommodation in North London. The police referred Mr N to Victim Support. Mr N had been the victim of common assault by two youths.

Mr N had recently moved from a residential unit for those with mental illnesses, to supported accommodation. He lived in a large flat with two other service users and had settled in well. His keyworker saw him on a daily basis and assisted N with a number of tasks, including shopping.

Whilst in a local shop, Mr N had been pushed to the floor by the two young men and verbally abused. The shopkeeper contacted the police immediately and the two young men were arrested. Mr N's keyworker had contacted Victim Support, explaining that Mr N wanted advice from Victim Support regarding his Personal Impact Statement that he was going to make when he saw the police officer.

A volunteer met with Mr N and his keyworker and explained the purpose of the statement and how it might be used in court. The volunteer gave Mr N and his keyworker information about the Witness Service at the Magistrates Court and suggested they make contact there if Mr N was required to attend court.

After the court case the volunteer met with Mr N and discussed the outcome of the case and how he was now coping.

Key points to consider when working with victims of crime

- Has the victim reported the matter to the police? If not, this will affect any claims to the Criminal Injuries Compensation Authority.
- Has the victim been referred to Victim Support?
- Is the victim defined as a 'vulnerable' witness under one or both of The Victims' Code of Practice and the Youth Justice and Criminal Evidence Act 1999?
- If so, are 'special measures' appropriate and applied for under the Youth Justice and Criminal Evidence Act 1999?
- Is therapeutic support envisaged? If so, consider liaison with the Crown Prosecution Service.
- Has the victim given a Victim Personal Statement to the police?
- Is the victim eligible for Criminal Injuries Compensation? If so the local Victim Support can assist.
- Have all agencies within the criminal justice system followed the Victims' Code of Practice? If unsure, contact local Victim Support who will be able to advise and assist.

Useful contacts

www.victimsupport.org.uk
www.homeoffice.gov.uk
www.criminal-injuries-compensation
www.hmso.gov.uk/acts.htm

References

Audit Commission (2002) *Helping Victims and Witnesses: The Work of Victim Support*. London: Audit Commission.
Brown, H. Stein, J. and Turk, V. (1995) The sexual abuse of adults with learning disabilities. *Mental Handicap Research*. 8: 3–24.

Clare, I.C. and Gudjonsson, G.H. (1993) Interrogative suggestibility, confabulation and acquiescence in people with mild learning disabilities (mental handicap): implications for reliability during police interviewing. *British Journal of Clinical Psychology*. 32: 295–301.

Clare, I.C. and Murphy, G. (2001) Witnesses with learning disabilities. *British Journal of Learning Disabilities*. 29: 79–80.

DoH (2001) *Valuing People: A New Strategy for Learning Disability for the Twenty First Century*. London: DoH.

Elliot, R. (1998) *Vulnerable and Intimidated Witnesses: A Review of the Literature, Annex A, Speaking up for Justice*. Home Office Research and Statistics Directorate.

Farrell, G. and Pease, K. (1993) *Once Bitten, Twice Bitten: Repeat Victimisation and Its Implications for Crime Prevention*. Crime Prevention Unit series; paper no. 46, London: HMSO.

Friedman, L. and Tucker, S. (1997) Violence prevention through victim assistance. In Davis, R., Lurigio, A. and Skogan, W. (Eds.) *Victims of Crime*. 2nd edn. London: Sage.

The Guardian (2003) *Mental Health Patients More Likely to Suffer Violence*. Thursday January 30.

Holdaway, S. et al. (2001) *New Strategies to Address Youth Offending: The National Evaluation of the Pilot Youth Offending Teams*. London: HMSO.

Home Office (1996) *The Victims Charter*. London: HMSO.

Home Office (1998) *Speaking up for Justice: Report of the Interdepartmental Working Group on the Treatment of Vulnerable and Intimidated Witnesses in the Criminal Justice System*. London: HMSO.

Home Office (2001a) *The Victim Personal Statement Scheme*. London: HMSO.

Home Office (2001b) *Criminal Justice Business Plan 2002–2003*. London: HMSO.

Home Office (2002a) *Achieving Best Evidence in Criminal Proceedings: Guidance for Vulnerable or Intimidated Witnesses, including Children*. London: HMSO.

Home Office (2002b) *Justice for All*. London: HMSO.

Home Office (2002c) *Narrowing the Justice Gap: Consultative Document*. London: HMSO.

Home Office (2003) *The Victims' Code of Practice: Indicative Draft*. London: HMSO.

Home Office (2003a) *Restorative Justice: the Government's strategy (2003)* A consultation document on the Government's strategy on Restorative Justice. London: HMSO.

Home Office (2003b) *A New Deal for Victims and Witnesses: National Strategy to Deliver Improved Services*. London: HMSO.

Hoyle, C., Morgan, R. and Sanders, A. (1999) *The Victims Charter: An Evaluation of Pilot Projects*. London: HMSO.

Maguire, M. and Corbett, C. (1987) *The Effects of Crime and the Work of Victim Support Schemes*. Aldershot: Gower.

Marshall, T. (1999) *Restorative Justice: An Overview*. London: HMSO.

McCabe, A. and Ford, C. (2001) *Redressing the Balance: Crime and Mental Health – Final Report*. UK Public Health Association.

Mencap (1999) *Living in Fear*. London: Mencap.

Mencap (2001) *Bullying: Living in Fear*. Campaign Report, London: Mencap.

Newburn, T. et al. (2001) *The Introduction of Referral Orders into the Youth Justice System* (First Interim Report). London: HMSO.

Pease, K. (1998) *Repeat Victimisation: Taking Stock*. Crime detection and prevention series, paper 90. London: HMSO.

Reeves, H. and Mulley, K. (2000) The new status of victims in the UK: opportunities and threats. In Crawford, A. and Goodey, J. (Eds.) *Integrating a Victim Perspective within Criminal Justice: International Debates*. Dartmouth: Ashgate.

Robinson, G. (1996) *Victim-Offender Mediation: Limitations and Potentials*. Oxford: Oxford University Press.

Sanders, A., Creaton, J., Bird, S. and Weber, L. (1996) *Witnesses with Learning Disabilities*, Research Findings no. 44. London: Home Office Research and Statistics Directorate.

Scottish Executive (2002) *Vital Voices: Helping Vulnerable Witnesses Give Evidence*. Consultation Paper. Edinburgh: Scottish Executive Justice Department.

Simmons, J. and Dodd, T. (Eds.) (2003) *Crime in England and Wales 2002/03*. Home Office Statistical Bulletin 07/03. London: Home Office.

The Times (2003) *Those Who Make Victims Feel Safe Are Now at Risk*. November 18.

Victim Support (1995) *The Rights of Victims of Crime*: A policy paper. London: Victim Support.

Victim Support (1998) Unpublished Training Material. London: Victim Support.

Victim Support (2002) *Criminal Neglect: No Justice Beyond Criminal Justice*. London: Victim Support.

Victim Support (2003) Vulnerable witness initiative fills a service gap. *Victim Support Magazine*.

Williams, C. (1995) *Invisible Victims: Crime and Abuse Against People With Learning Difficulties*. London: Jessica Kingsley.

Williams, B. (1999) *Working with Victims of Crime: Policies, Politics and Practice*. London: Jessica Kingsley.

Wilson, C. and Brewer, N. (1992) The incidence of criminal victimisation of individuals with an intellectual disability. *Australian Psychologist*. 27: 114–7.

Chapter 4

The Detention of Mentally Disordered Offenders under the Mental Health Act 1983

Soo Lee and Julia Warrener

Introduction

One key crossover point between the criminal justice and mental health systems is when someone who has committed a criminal offence is judged to be mentally disordered, and is detained under mental health legislation in psychiatric provision.

This chapter will provide an account of the legal means by which people with mental health problems can be detained under the Mental Health Act 1983 (MHA, 1983) (DHSS, 1983) in these circumstances, and then will consider the nature and effects of such detention. The MHA 1983 is a complex piece of legislation, which like other such pieces of legislation, has been subject to a great deal of interpretation through the courts leading to a significant body of case law. Readers who wish to pursue these issues in more depth can consult other published literature for further insight into the use of the Act, such as *Mental Health Act Manual* (Jones, 2004). The next chapter in this book, *Life under Detention in Psychiatric Provision*, will examine different treatment resources and how the mental health system can compound disadvantage for individuals.

There are three routes to detention for mentally disordered offenders under mental health legislation. Two of these are through the courts; the crown court, and the Magistrates' court. The third route is through the Parliamentary Executive, where the Home Secretary can direct that the person be detained in psychiatric provisions. The following section sets out the legislation that is applied in these circumstances.

An outline of the relevant provisions of the legislation

The current MHA 1983 (DHSS, 1983) inherited several aspects of the previous 1959 Mental Health Act. The major changes have been the emphasis on the protection of rights of detained patients, and the duty to provide aftercare services. These changes are reflected in the various provisions of the 1983 Act and the relevant parts that concern the detention, care and treatment of mentally disordered offenders are as follows:

- Part I outlines the application of the Act.
- Part III refers to powers of the courts and the Home Secretary.
- Part IV relates to consent to treatment.
- Part V concerns Mental Health Review Tribunals.

The next section sets out these powers as appropriate to mentally disordered offenders.

Part I of the Mental Health Act 1983

Application of the Act

The application of the Act concerns all patients subject to detention including mentally disordered offenders. The application of one or more of the four specific classifications that embrace the definition of mental disorder must be a precursor to any detention.

In the 1983 Act, mental disorder means:

- mental illness
- mental impairment
- severe mental impairment
- psychopathic disorder

The term mental illness is undefined in English law and each individual case is mainly left to clinical judgement (DHSS, 1987). However, Jones provides further guidance and states that mental illness means an illness having one or more of the following characteristics:

- *More than temporary impairment of intellectual functions shown by a failure of memory, orientation, comprehension and learning capacity.*
- *More than temporary alteration of mood of such degree as to give rise to the patient having a delusional appraisal of his situation, his past or his future, or that of others or to the lack of any appraisal.*
- *Delusional beliefs, persecutory, jealous or grandiose.*
- *Abnormal perceptions associated with delusional misinterpretation of events; thinking so disordered as to prevent the patient making a*

reasonable appraisal of his situation or having reasonable communication with others.

(Jones, 2004)

The guidance offered above complies with the descriptions in the International Classification of Diseases (ICD) (World Health Organisation (WHO) 1992). The lack of any official definition of mental illness may, at times, lead to the criticism that it can be over-inclusive in relation to certain people's disturbances and types of behaviours, and how these are interpreted as psychiatric disorders.

To justify the use of the terms for mental impairment and severe mental impairment, there are two components. First, there has to be evidence of 'a state of arrested or incomplete development of mind'. This is usually confirmed by psychometric testing. Secondly, there has to be evidence associated with abnormally aggressive behaviour or seriously irresponsible conduct. The terms used have largely been inherited from the 1959 Act (Jones, 2004). The distinction between mental impairment and severe mental impairment is one of degree: the impairment of intelligence and social functioning is significant in the former and severe in the latter. These definitions are intended to protect people with a learning disability and ensure that they are not subject to long-term compulsory detention unless their behaviour warrants it (DHSS, 1987). However, the consideration of the boundary between whether or when a condition is significant or severe is, again, left to clinical judgement.

The Code of Practice (DoH, 1999) is an important document as it provides guidance to mental health professionals about how the MHA 1983 should be implemented and interpreted. All practice within mental health settings and by mental health professionals should adhere to the guidelines set out in the Code of Practice (DoH, 1999). Paragraphs 30.5 and 30.6 of the Code of Practice (DoH, 1999) provide further guidance in the interpretation of the terms of abnormally aggressive behaviour or seriously irresponsible conduct. Examples of the former include causing damage or real distress, and in the latter, showing a lack of responsibility or disregard of the consequences of the actions taken.

Much of the definition of psychopathic disorder has remained intact from the 1959 Act. There must be a persistent disorder or disability of mind, resulting in abnormally aggressive or seriously irresponsible behaviour, whether or not including significant impairment of intelligence. Being persistent implies that it has been in existence for a considerable time (DHSS, 1987). Whilst the issue of treatability of this condition is not included in the definition, it is an essential point for consideration when patients are admitted for compulsory treatment, i.e. under section 37 or 47 in the case of mentally disordered offenders (see relevant sections later in this chapter for further details of these). There have been numerous discussion papers on the nature and treatment options of psychopathic disorder (see for example, Butler Report, Home Office and DHSS, 1975; DoH and Home Office, 1994; DoH, 1999a) but it is beyond the remit of this chapter to critique the subject.

Part I of the Act makes clear that persons with a mental disorder cannot be detained and treated compulsorily solely on the grounds of sexual deviancy, promiscuous immoral conduct, alcohol or drug misuse. Nonetheless, it is possible to detain someone with problems of substance misuse if the manifestation coexists with mental disorder. However, if the individual is under the influence of an intoxicating substance at the point of assessment, the assessment should be delayed unless it was not possible because of the urgency of the situation or the person's behaviour, (DoH, 1999). It is essential that the professionals involved obtain a clear and objective picture of an individual's mental health problems, separate from the influence of any intoxicating substance (DoH, 1999).

Having considered the required grounds for detention of mentally disordered offenders under the MHA 1983, it is also necessary to consider the relevant sections of the 1983 Act which pertain to admission and the likely venues for the treatment of mentally disordered offenders. Part III of the Act defines the process by which mentally disordered offenders are admitted and detained in hospital.

Summary

- There are three routes to detention for mentally disordered offenders; crown court; Magistrate' court; from prison on the direction of the Home Secretary.
- An individual must be detained under one of four classifications; either mental illness or mental impairment or severe mental impairment or psychopathic disorder.
- The Code of Practice provides official guidance for all professionals implementing the MHA (1983).

Case study 1

Mr B is a African-Caribbean young man. He has a long history of psychotic illness and has had several admissions to mental health services under the Mental Health Act 1983.

He has attended the hospital without any prior appointment on more than one occasion asking for help. He was hearing voices and could not cope with it any more as the voices were getting more unpleasant. He was told to go away and visit his GP, as the service would only accept referrals from his GP.

He went home but the voices did not abate. He set fire to his flat as the voices had commanded. This sequence of events led to him being detained in a secure hospital.

The plight of this young man, who did not have a forensic history until this point, and the lack of a positive response to his call for help could have prevented his subsequent admission to a secure setting, and excluded him from having a forensic record.

This case study demonstrates that good risk assessment can be therapeutic and work in the interest of the patient. However, implementing an inflexible and insensitive system could have a profound impact on the overall well-being of mental health patients, disadvantaging them even further.

Powers of the courts and the Home Secretary – Part III of the Mental Health Act 1983

This part of the Act deals with circumstances in which mentally disordered individuals may be admitted to and detained in hospital or received into guardianship on the order of a court, or may be transferred to a hospital or guardianship from penal institutions on the direction of the Home Secretary.

There has been a trend towards diverting mentally disordered offenders to hospitals from the penal system. Diversion requires multi-agency or multi-professional working and effective communication across health, criminal justice and welfare systems. The problems and difficulties associated with multi-agency and multi-professional working cannot be under estimated, and government guidance is available (DoH, 1996). The interface between the MHA 1983, the Human Rights Act (HRA) (1998) and other criminal justice legislation must be clearly understood by all professionals who work with mentally disordered offenders.

The rights of individuals are protected in each of the eight Articles of the Human Rights Act 1998. The incorporation of the Human Rights Act 1998 into United Kingdom law has had consequences for both new and existing legislation, such as the Mental Health Act 1983, as all legislation must now be compatible with the strictures of the Human Rights Act 1998. Existing legislation can be challenged in a court of law if there is a case where legislation does not comply with the provisions of the Human Rights Act 1998. Moreover, the practice of mental health professionals particularly and psychiatric institutions in general, can be challenged legally if it does not comply with the provisions of the Human Rights Act 1998. The impact of the Human Rights Act 1998 will be considered in greater detail later in this chapter.

Remands for psychiatric reports are used to provide an alternative to prison department remands when bail is considered inappropriate in the circumstances. The court is empowered to remand an accused or convicted offender to hospital for the purpose of:

- Preparation of a medical report on his mental condition (section 35).
- Treatment (section 36).
- Being received into guardianship (section 37).
- An interim order (section 38).

Preparation of medical report

Section 35 of the MHA allows for the remand of an accused person to hospital in order for a medical report to be prepared and therefore enables a thorough assessment of the individual's mental state to be undertaken. Section 35 is appropriate where it would not be practicable to remand the person on bail, especially when the accused might be likely to break the condition of bail. (Bail is the commitment made by the person accused of an offence to be present at trial at a later date. Bail is usually secured by money or property.) An initial 28 day order may be made and may last up to a maximum of 12 weeks, on condition that the court is satisfied that arrangements for the accused to be admitted to hospital within a period of seven days beginning with the date of the remand can be made. The hospital also needs to be able to provide an appropriate level of security, as a place of safety is of paramount importance.

Patients remanded under section 35 may not be subject to Part IV of the Act, i.e. treatment. Treatment may only be administered in an emergency under common law. This anomaly has led to the practice of 'dual detention' of remand patients, i.e. being on a civil detention order at the same time, in order that treatment is followed by assessment (Mental Health Act Commission 1999). The legality of such practice is documented in Jones (1996, 5th edn. para. 1–324).

Whilst subject to section 35, the accused remains under the jurisdiction of the remanding court. There is no provision for the hospital to grant leave of absence or to transfer to another hospital without the consent of the court. Problems arise when the patient requires medical attention at another hospital or requests compassionate leave. If the patient absconds, they may be arrested without a warrant by any constable and appear again before the remanding court (DHSS, 1987).

Remand for treatment

Section 36 of the Act allows the court to issue an order for remanding the accused to hospital for treatment, on the evidence of two medical practitioners that the accused is suffering from a mental disorder of a nature or degree that makes it appropriate for them to be detained in hospital for treatment. This is in contrast to section 35 where a diagnosis of mental disorder has not yet been established. Similar remand conditions apply as in section 35 with the exception of Part IV of the Act, to which the accused is subject as they are admitted for the purpose of treatment.

Issue of guardianship order

As an alternative to a penal disposal, the court may employ section 37 and issue a hospital or guardianship order. This will be on the evidence of two medical practitioners, and is for the accused person found to be suffering from a mental disorder at the time of sentencing. The court has to be satisfied that the offender is suffering from mental illness, mental impairment, severe mental impairment or psychopathic disorder; and that either disorder is of a nature or degree that makes it appropriate for them to be detained in hospital for treatment, within a 28 day period.

Once admitted to hospital, a hospital order patient has the same rights as a patient detained under civil detention, in relation to the provisions of the Act; i.e. consent to treatment, leave of absence, right of appeal against detention to a Mental Health Review Tribunal, and the right to aftercare arrangements. The order may be renewed as in the MHA section 1983 and discharged by the responsible medical officer (RMO) at any time. The RMO is defined in section 34 as the doctor in charge of treatment of the patient. Legally, it does not have to be the consultant psychiatrist, although this would be normal practice. In the absence of the consultant psychiatrist, there must be a delegated person fulfilling the role in the interim. A patient can only have one doctor acting as the RMO at any one time, whilst detained under the MHA 1983. Where a patient is subject to guardianship, the RMO is authorised by social services.

In relation to guardianship under section 37, the court may confer the local authority or a named person to act as guardian to the offender. The powers and effects of the guardianship are those set out in sections 7 and 8 of the Act. The offender may be required to reside at a specific place; and attend specific places for occupation, treatment, education or training. The offender may have to give access to the responsible medical officer, an approved social worker or any other person as specified. The guidance in the Code of Practice (DoH, 1999) should be followed when considering ordering guardianship under section 37.

Issue of interim order

An interim order under section 38 may be issued by the court to convicted offenders on the evidence of two medical practitioners that the offender is suffering from one or more of the four classifications of mental disorder. The intention is to evaluate the offender's response in hospital before a hospital order is made. An initial 12 week order may be made, and this may be extended by further periods of no more than 28 days on each subsequent occasion. The total duration of the interim order may not last beyond 12 months.

For offenders under section 38, Part IV of the Act applies and they remain under the jurisdiction of the remanding court; therefore there is no provision for leave of absence without recourse to the court.

Summary

Courts are empowered to remand an accused or convicted offender to hospital for either the preparation of a psychiatric report, treatment, or the assessment of an individual's mental health needs.

Power of the court to restrict discharge

Following a hospital disposal under section 37, and having regard to the nature of the offence, the antecedents of the offender and the likelihood of them committing a further offence if discharged from hospital, a crown court may impose a restriction order under section 41 with or without time limit, for the purpose of the protection of the public from serious harm (DHSS, 1987). In its deliberations, at least one of the medical recommendations given to the court must be taken into account.

A Magistrates' court does not have the power to impose a restriction order but may commit the offender to the crown court under section 43 of the Act. Section 44 of the Act provides direction for the Magistrates' court under a hospital order, pending a hearing by the crown court.

Section 41 has the effect of restricting discharge from the hospital, transfer of the offender to another hospital and of granting leave of absence from the hospital without the consent of the Home Secretary. The Home Secretary has the power to terminate the restriction order at any time. The powers of the Home Secretary in respect of patients subject to restriction orders are set out in section 42 of the Act. A patient subject to a restriction order has the right to appeal to a Mental Health Review Tribunal (MHRT) for discharge either conditionally, with community supervision, or absolutely.

Summary

Section 41 of the Act imposes a discharge restriction on a Hospital Order (section 37) and has the purpose of protecting the public from serious harm. All major clinical decisions, i.e. transfer between hospitals, have to have consent of the Home Secretary.

Persons to be detained during Her Majesty's Pleasure

Under section 46, the Home Secretary may direct, by warrant, the detention to hospital of a current serviceman in the armed forces. The direction has the same effect of a hospital order together with a restriction order.

Transfer of prisoners to hospitals

The MHA 1983 also makes provision for the transfer of remand and convicted prisoners to a psychiatric hospital. The provisions of sections 47 to 53 empower the Home Secretary to transfer prisoners suffering from mental disorder from penal institutions to hospitals. Different considerations apply to sentenced and remand prisoners. This is because ultimately the latter need to be brought before a court to resolve the proceedings in which they are involved.

Section 47 has the same effect as a court order, and is sometimes known as a 'notional section 37'. This is where the prisoner is directed to detention in hospital for treatment, based on two medical reports. However, prisoners whose sentences end whilst being detained under the MHA 1983 can continue to be detained under compulsory powers in hospital if it is deemed necessary for the individual's health, safety, or protection of others. The Home Secretary may impose a transfer restriction under section 49 so that the patient may not be discharged, sent on leave or transferred to another hospital without their consent. The restriction order ceases when the period of prison sentence ends.

Applying the same requirements and having the same effect as section 47, remand prisoners may be transferred to hospital under section 48. It may be appropriate to impose a restriction order under section 49 for prisoners detained in a prison or remand centre and those remanded in custody by a Magistrates' court. The Home Secretary may exercise their discretion on whether to impose a restriction order for civil prisoners other than those covered by the Immigration Acts. In most cases, the remand prisoner may not have been tried and convicted. If the responsible medical officer believes that the patient is not fit to return to court, the court may, under section 51(5) direct a hospital order in their absence without convicting them. Under the provisions of section 51, the transfer direction and the restriction order cease to have effect when the case has been fully dealt with by the court. The transfer direction also ceases to have effect when the period of remand expires unless he is further remanded.

Following notification by the hospital or the Mental Health Review Tribunal, under section 50, the Home Secretary is informed that the sentenced prisoner/patient no longer requires hospital treatment; he may direct that the patient be returned to prison to serve the remaining sentence or direct a discharge from hospital on the same terms as he would be released from prison.

Summary

Prisoners can be transferred from prison to hospital, at the direction of the Home Secretary, under section 47. A section 49 may be applied, which is a discharge restriction order similar in operation to section 41

- Any of sections 35, 36, 37, with or without a restriction order (section 41), and 38 can be applied in order for a mentally disordered offender to receive either a psychiatric assessment in hospital or psychiatric treatment under the MHA 1983.
- Section 47 allows for the transfer of a sentenced prisoner to hospital with or without a restriction i.e. under section 49. Section 48 allows for the transfer of a remand prisoner to a psychiatric hospital.

The rights of detained individuals – Part V of the Mental Health Act 1983

The processes open to individuals to challenge the power implicit in the mental health system and promote their rights as individuals are now considered. These include:

- Legal representation.
- Mental Health Review Tribunals (MHRT), with reference to the impact of the Human Rights Act 1998 (HRA) on the operation of the MHRT system.
- Advocacy services open to detained individuals.

The role of the Mental Health Act Commission (MHAC) and advocacy services open to detained individuals, are considered in Chapter 5, *Life under Detention in Psychiatric Provision*.

It is important to acknowledge that mentally disordered offenders who are admitted to secure hospital require legal representation. It is common for individuals to have two solicitors, one to work with any outstanding criminal issues, specifically relevant for those retained under section 38 of the MHA 1983, and one qualified to represent them within the mental health system. The mentally disordered offender is able to instruct their solicitor at any time during an admission in order for them to advocate on their behalf about relevant issues, for example where they feel their rights have been infringed or where they are dissatisfied with an aspect of their care and treatment. However, it is crucially important for the individual to receive qualified legal advice and representation at a Mental Health Review Tribunal (MHRT).

Section 66 of the MHA 1983 stipulates the patient's right of appeal, against their detention, to a MHRT. A mentally disordered offender is entitled to apply for a MHRT, within the time frames stipulated by the MHA 1983 during their detention. It is also important to acknowledge that mentally disordered offenders are guaranteed an automatic review of their detention, via the MHRT, if they have not applied for one themselves within the previous three years. The individual's nearest relative within the meaning of the Act can also apply for a MHRT on the person's behalf.

The MHRT is a three-member body, comprised of a legal, medical and lay member, all of whom are from the hospital: it has the specific purpose of reviewing an individual's independent detention under the 1983 Act. Ultimately the Tribunal has power to discharge absolutely, or defer discharge until their stipulated conditions are met, if all members agree that this is appropriate. The Tribunal takes written and oral evidence from the individual's RMO and social worker. The person's solicitor, on their behalf, is able to question both professionals on their reasons for continued detention under the 1983 Act and advocate for the person's discharge from a detention order and at times from hospital. Legal representation at MHRT, whilst not compulsory as the person can represent themselves if they so wish, is vital in the authors' opinions for the detained person. The MHRT functions as a judicial review and it is extremely important that the individual has a professional advocate to challenge the power and professional imbalances implicit in such a situation.

The incorporation of the European Convention on Human Rights 1998 (ECHR) into UK law by way of the Human Rights Act 1998 (HRA) in October 2000 was viewed as a significant milestone. However, research demonstrates that perhaps the introduction of the HRA has not had the overwhelming impact it was first hoped. Home Office (2001) figures suggest that of 297 court cases analysed from 2/10/00, only 56 resulted in a HRA claim being upheld or only 18.9 per cent of cases.

However, the HRA has had an important bearing upon certain aspects of the mental health system allowing challenges to current legislation. The ECHR has decreed that for detention under the MHA 1983 to comply with the convention and therefore be legal it must be compatible with Article 5 and protect against arbitrary detention. The disorder, therefore, must be established by medical evidence, be persistent and be of a 'nature or degree warranting compulsory confinement'. Moreover, the detained individual must have access to a speedy review of their detention by an independent body.

The HRA has enabled individuals to challenge the mental health system where the system has appeared to infringe their human rights. Two important issues will be highlighted in more detail, these being burden of proof and the entitlement to a speedy independent review.

Case study 2

Mr E was initially detained in one of the three high security hospitals for some years and later transferred to a medium secure unit where he applied to the Mental Health Review Tribunal for an absolute discharge from a section 37/41 order. The detention order was imposed following his offence when he fatally assaulted two of his partner's infant children, using a knife, machete and hammer, and making a murderous attack on the mother of the children with a hammer. It was submitted that at the time of the offence, the patient was intoxicated with alcohol.

The diagnosis was one of psychopathic disorder, but there had not been any evidence of mental illness or a need for psychiatric medication. It was clear that during the years of hospitalisation, Mr E had shown no signs of any aggressive or destructive behaviour. He had not participated in the activities provided; his contact with nursing staff and other patients on the ward had been minimal and he spent time in his room by himself when not out on leave, as he did not perceive any of these were helpful to him. He turned down the offer of help to address the issue of alcohol as he claimed that he had completed a number of alcohol education courses at the previous hospital. However, he had had ongoing sessions with the clinical psychologist. His frequent and lengthy unescorted leave in the community had taken place without any untoward incidents. There had been no evidence of any resumption of alcohol intake.

Despite years of hospitalisation in a secure setting, Mr E had retained his overall functioning and had not required supervision from staff other than the need to inform staff of his general whereabouts as he was a detained patient. Mr E resented having to account for his movements to staff when he returned from leave on each occasion. Whilst there was support for conditional discharge from the clinical team, Mr E's advocate and independent opinion was providing evidence for an absolute discharge. The clinical team had therefore pursued seeking supervised accommodation locally so that the same team could continue the statutory supervision required following conditional discharge. The Home Office voiced their concern should Mr E's mental state deteriorate again.

An important issue to address was whether Mr E was still suffering from a psychopathic disorder or had a persistent disorder of mind that results in abnormally aggressive behaviour. Given that the burden of proof was on the detaining authority (following the implementation of the Human Rights Act 1998) and their support for conditional discharge, this implied that further detention for hospital treatment was no longer appropriate. However, there was the counter argument that living independently would make Mr E susceptible to all of life's stresses, therefore rendering Mr E vulnerable after discharge. The concern was that Mr E's potential for abusing alcohol as a coping mechanism would be greater, resulting in abnormally aggressive behaviour.

Mr E was adamant that he had learnt to cope whilst in hospital, as it was the most stressful place he had lived in, and that the leave periods had demonstrated that he could manage community living without any formal support or follow up. He had made plans to involve himself in mental health voluntary organisations.

Would continued detention be of greater risk due to Mr E's high level of frustration that might lead to an escalation into alcohol and psychopathic tendencies? What about the issue of public safety? Should the patient be liable to recall? The burden of proof for continued detention is a balance of probability as no one can be absolutely certain about the future behaviour of Mr E.

This case study seeks to highlight the tension between risk assessment, the welfare of the patient and public safety. Whilst Mr E had shown that his behaviour had been impeccable during the years of hospitalisation, his offence had become an issue in respect of public safety when he applied for an absolute discharge. Given that there is no crystal ball that could predict the future and the life stresses that may face Mr E, there was the necessity to put safety nets in place to reduce or minimise the risks. In this case, conditional discharge with a number of conditions, including the type of accommodation, statutory supervision and the liability to recall, would suffice.

This case study also demonstrates that the mental health system can be more punitive than the penal system. If Mr E were to serve a prison sentence for the offence committed, he would be released when the sentence came to an end. The conditional discharge of the section 37/41 meant that he would be subject to supervision and recall.

As stated above legal detention has to be based upon clear objective medical evidence. When an individual is first assessed for possible detention, the two medical practitioners have to demonstrate and recommend grounds for admission providing evidence that the individual suffers from a mental disorder. The burden of proof is with the professionals to demonstrate that admission is necessary. However, prior to the HRA detained individuals had to demonstrate to the MHRT that discharge was appropriate and that they were no longer in need of treatment; the burden of proof therefore lay with the individual to prove that they were ready for discharge. In a legal challenge to this situation, in March of 2001 (*R.(H)* v. *MHRT, North and East London Region* and another from *www.markwalton.net*) it was found that this process, as defined in sections 72 and 73 of the Mental Health Act (1983) was incompatible with Article 5. As a consequence the burden of proof has subsequently been reversed, and so now in both their written and oral evidence to the MHRT the professionals must demonstrate the need for the individual's continued detention.

Delays within the MHRT system have been well documented, and attributed to many factors, not least of which is a scarcity of Tribunal members, coupled with a demand for increasing numbers of Tribunals. Recent legal challenges to these delays have proven that the human rights of individuals have been breached, i.e. in relation to Article 5.4 of the HRA, which requires the lawfulness of a detention to be decided speedily by a Court (*KB* et al. v. *MHRT*, and *Sec of State 2001 and R (C)* v. *MHRT* 03/07/01 (*www.markwalton.net*). As a result of such case law the responsibility of the state to facilitate a 'speedy review' of individuals' detention is clear, with recommendations that the Government must now 'provide such resources as will provide a speedy hearing'.

The rights of appeal of individuals detained under the MHA 1983 are protected by the MHRT system. The incorporation of the ECHR into UK law has resulted in some proactive challenges to the Tribunal system, with positive outcomes for the progression and empowerment of individuals detained within the mental health system. However, there is an apparent need for practice within psychiatric institutions to be proactively, as opposed to reactively, framed by the HRA, for the on-going empowerment of detained individuals.

Having considered possible routes in to hospital within the framework provided by the MHA 1983 and the legal rights of detainees in relation to these, it is also necessary to consider different treatment resources and how the mental health system impacts on individuals, which can compound disadvantage. These issues are dealt with in the following chapter.

References

DHSS (1983) *Mental Health Act 1983*. London: HMSO.

DHSS (1987) *Mental Health Act 1983. Memorandum on Parts I to VI, VIII and X*. London: HMSO.

DoH and Home Office (1994) *Report of the Department of Health and Home Office Working Group on Psychopathic Disorder*. London: Department of Health.

DoH (1996) *Building Bridges.* London: The Stationery Office.
DoH (1999) *Mental Health Act 1983: Code of Practice.* London: The Stationery Office.
DoH (1999a) *Report of the Committee of Inquiry into the Personality Disorder Unit, Ashworth Hospital.* London: The Stationery Office.
Home Office and DHSS (1975) *Report of the Committee on Mental Abnormal Offenders* (Butler Report). Cmnd. 6244, London: HMSO.
Home Office (2001) *The Human Rights Act Research Unit,* Lord Chancellor's Department, www.lcd.gov.uk/hract/hramenu.htm
Jones, R. (1996) *Mental Health Act Manual.* 5th edn. London: Sweet & Maxwell.
Jones, R. (2004) *Mental Health Act Manual.* 8th edn. London: Sweet & Maxwell.
World Health Organisation (1992) *The ICD–10 Classification of Mental and Behavioural Disorders. Clinical Descriptions and Diagnostic Guidelines.* Geneva: World Health Organisation.

Chapter 5

Life under Detention in Psychiatric Provision

Soo Lee, Steve Cloudsdale and Julia Warrener

Introduction

In the last chapter, the legal provisions for the detention of people with mental disorders, who have also committed criminal offences, were considered. This chapter now examines the types of resources and treatments that can be utilised for such people.

Mentally disordered offenders can receive treatment in psychiatric intensive care units (PICUs) operating within general psychiatry, but are more likely to be admitted to forensic services, i.e. secure hospitals. In order to examine the impact of detention upon the lives of individuals it is necessary to consider the issue both from the structural and individual perspective, with specific attention to how the mental health system can compound disadvantage for detained individuals. The following sections will consequently offer a definition of secure hospital services, review their development and consider the impact of such services on the lives of individuals.

Previous research demonstrates the connection between severe and enduring mental illness and levels of acute social deprivation and disadvantage (Glover et al., 1999; Lelliott et al., 2001). It is extremely likely that individuals admitted to secure hospital have experienced considerable disadvantage both in socio-economic terms and in the context of their personal lives. Many have endured traumatic experiences often without access to professional help and support. It is apparent that the ways in which secure (i.e. locked) forensic services have developed in the UK possibly compounds disadvantage for individuals.

Defining secure services; reviewing their development

How do we define secure hospital settings? Environmental security is obviously important, and requires perimeter security, secure systems of entry and exit to the hospital or particular wards and security within wards to maintain safety and manage risk. Environmental security is then complemented by procedural and relational security (DoH, 2000). Procedural security refers to the policies and protocols required to enable the hospital and wards within it to function with the appropriate degree of consistency and safety for both detained individuals and staff. Relational security is concerned with the degree of security required within the individual's relationship with staff. Relational security is achieved through appropriate staffing ratios and by mechanisms, such as staff supervision and mentoring, which aim to ensure the therapeutic effectiveness of the relationship between individuals and staff. Secure hospitals within the UK maintain, to a higher or lesser degree, environmental, procedural and relational security. There could be an apparent contradiction between the focus upon security and secure systems and the need to provide a therapeutic environment for detained individuals. However, as Robinson and Kettles (2000) have argued 'a secure environment is required to act as a basis for and to enable all psychotherapeutic work to take place'. Secure hospital provision is provided on three levels: high security, i.e. highly secure hospitals, those more commonly known as Broadmoor, Rampton and Ashworth; medium secure hospitals; and low security care, either within acute settings or rehabilitation venues provided by the National Health Service (NHS) and the independent sector.

The history of the secure services demonstrates that development has been piecemeal across regions (Mullen, 2000). The various schemes in operation for mentally disordered offenders to be diverted away from the criminal justice system compound the situation. This has led to inequality in provision, with under-provision in some authorities. The consequent gaps in services can have detrimental effects on the lives of those requiring secure care; for example, an individual may have to be admitted to a secure hospital some distance from their home if no appropriate service exists in their area. This is inevitably disorientating for the individual and leads to them feeling isolated; isolation which is compounded if family and friends are unable to visit due to the distances involved or possible financial constraints. It has also been argued that long distance admissions can increase the individual's sense of illness, and has echoes of:

. . . the 'big house on the hill' image that psychiatry was meant to have left behind.

(Maden, 2001)

Criticisms have also been levelled at the lack of integration between secure hospital services and community based provision (Mullen, 2000). It has been claimed therefore that communications between providers of services are unclear, which frequently leads to lengthy and complicated transfer negotiations. This again can have a negative impact on the individual, extending the duration of an individual's admission inappropriately to their identified needs. Inter-agency collaborative working is essential to facilitate a smooth transition of care (DoH, 1996).

It has been well documented that referral rates to secure psychiatric provision are escalating, with increasing numbers of individuals admitted under Part III of the MHA 1983 as detailed earlier in this chapter (Hotopf et al., 2000). Such increases have been ascribed to increasing concerns about the need to manage risk to the general public, led by government policy and compounded by media coverage on mental health care and the consequent reluctance of professionals to work creatively with risk (Hotopf et al., 2000). Rose (1998) has argued that such practice has been one of the main precipitating factors for the expansion of forensic services during the last 20 years. Moreover, he suggests that new forensic units are defined more by their need to provide secure environments rather than the need to provide therapy and care. Why has this emphasis upon risk assessment occurred and is it a valid basis for service provision? Does it further disadvantage mentally disordered offenders detained in secure hospitals?

Risk assessment and risk management

There has been a political and social policy shift with regard to the way we perceive and understand mental health problems. The language of risk assessment and risk management now pervades mental health in the UK (Rose, 1998). It is apparent that this policy shift has occurred as a result of the closure of the large psychiatric institutions and the perceived and well-publicised 'failure' of community care to prevent harm to themselves and others by those who have evident mental health problems (BBC Online, 08/12/98). However, research demonstrates that there has not been an increase in the number of homicides committed by individuals with mental health problems since the policy of community care was instituted (Taylor and Gunn, 1999). Concern for public safety, although obviously important, has been seen to take political precedence over the welfare of those living with mental health problems.

The focus upon risk assessment and management is intended to invite more objective and robust analysis (Duggan, 1997), with the aim of reducing the risk of violent incidents by mentally disordered individuals. However, is it possible to promote the interests of detained individuals and of the general public solely through a focus upon risk assessment? Munro and Rumgay (2000) have argued that improving professionals' ability to assess risk is unlikely to lead to increased safety for the public. Improving accuracy is difficult and they suggest that it is unrealistic to expect risk assessments to achieve high accuracy.

We would suggest that the focus upon risk within mental health services in the UK adds to the disadvantage experienced by mentally disordered offenders. Firstly, as others have argued, the focus upon risk increases the stigma faced by mentally disordered offenders (Petch, 2001). Representations of mentally disordered offenders in the media automatically connect the mentally disordered with risk, crime and harm to others (Cutcliffe, 2001). Secondly, in such a climate, which is legitimised politically and through social policy mechanisms, mental health professionals may exercise caution with regard to working creatively with individuals. As has been previously suggested, this encourages defensive practice. A consequence of this may be that the threshold for professional intervention may be lowered, with the increased potential for the assessment and detention of those who are actually of lesser risk (Munro and Rumgay, 2000). In relation to assessing and managing risk of those detained in secure hospitals the impact of a low threshold for risk could prolong an individual's admission over and above their level of need. Finally, the focus on risk assessment and risk management has the potential to relegate care and treatment within mental health services to a secondary process. Mentally disordered offenders detained under the MHA 1983 are entitled to expect positive outcomes for the treatment of their mental health problems and not solely a focus on their risk to themselves or others or their projected rate of recidivism.

It is important, therefore, to promote effective mental health services, which focus on the care and treatment of individuals as an organic way of reducing risk to themselves or others. High standards of care are essential if we are to promote the mental health of detained individuals, challenge disadvantage and avert disaster (Petch, 2001).

Ethnicity issues

Within the increasing numbers of individuals detained within the secure hospital system there is an over representation of both men and women from minority ethnic communities, and this is especially true of women and men of black African Caribbean origin (Lelliott et al., 2001). The Reed Report (DoH/Home Office, 1992) highlighted a number of pertinent issues with regard to the experience of individuals from ethnic minority communities within the mental health system, not least of which is that black African Caribbean individuals are more likely to be detained in secure facilities. The historical perspective of the forced migration of African Caribbean people during the slavery period, the traumatic experience of subsequent migration to this country, and the disruptive effects these have had on their offspring have been reported as major issues affecting the mental health and well being of African Caribbean people. The current system of mental health care has also been reported as not being at all sensitive to the different needs of black people (Aiyegbusi, 2000).

Gender issues

Women are also proportionally over represented within secure accommodation in general, and it is noted that women's detention in secure accommodation is frequently inappropriate, with women often placed in levels of security that are too high for their acknowledged need (DoH, 2000). It seems apparent that a sporadically planned and largely non-integrated service will struggle to meet the specific needs of an increasingly diverse population. The constant criticism of current secure care for women has been well documented (DoH, 2002).

It is clear therefore that the way the secure hospital system has developed in the UK has an apparent detrimental impact upon the way individuals detained within it experience the system. The structure and processes of the secure hospital system appear to compound disadvantage for individuals rather than alleviate or challenge it. However, it is also important to consider how the detail of life within a secure hospital impacts upon the lives of individuals. The experiences of individuals within the secure hospital system are wide-ranging. In an effort to offer a general picture of the impact of such a system on the lives of individuals, the issues will be considered in relation to two key themes: the ways in which the system may compound disadvantage for individuals, and their rights within the system.

Summary

- There is a proven link between severe and enduring mental health issues and acute social deprivation.
- Secure hospitals are defined in terms of environmental, procedural and relational security.
- It is apparent that the way secure forensic services have developed impacts upon the lives of those detained within them.
- There is an over representation of minority groups detained under the MHA 1983 and within secure services.

Impact on the individual

The different types of security that define a secure hospital have already been outlined (high, low and medium security). Prior to, and on admission, an individual will obviously be made aware of the way in which the ward or unit operates, the treatments and interventions available and the processes by which the mental health system attempts to ensure that their treatment needs are met and continually reviewed. This may be, for example, through regular consultation with members of the clinical team and through regular Care Programme Approach (CPA) reviews (DoH, 1999b). The individual will also be informed of their rights under the MHA 1983. How does the process of admission impact upon the lives of individuals?

One major area where an individual will lack the opportunity to determine their own choices centres upon treatment. It is not possible for us to outline the various treatments in any detail here, and treatment interventions are covered in other literature; e.g. Clare (1998) and Hodgins and Miller-Isberner (2000). One of the key issues to raise is the individual's inability to exercise choice with regard to treatment in general. Individuals are detained under the MHA 1983 to receive treatment for their mental health needs or for assessment followed by treatment. Part IV of the Mental Health Act details provision with regard to the treatment of detained individuals.

Consent to treatment

Chapters 15 and 16 of the Code of Practice (Department of Health, 1999) also provide guidance in respect to consent to treatment. The Mental Health Act Commission (MHAC) biennial reports offer discussion and a general overview on the operational issues involved in exercising the powers and duties in respect to consent to treatment by hospital staff.

For mentally disordered offenders detained in hospital for treatment, the hospital is obliged to make available information regarding treatment and what informed consent means. The MHA allows treatment to be given without consent during the first three months (Department of Health, 1999) after which time the responsible medical officer (RMO) is obliged to negotiate consent for treatment. A record of when consent was being negotiated should be made in the clinical notes along with the content of discussion in respect to the nature, purpose and the likely effects of the proposed treatment. If the patient refuses treatment considered necessary for their disorder, a second opinion must be sought. The patient would have to comply with the treatment if the second opinion doctor, appointed by the MHAC, issues a certificate of second opinion (Form 39). The independent doctor has a duty to interview the individual, consult with the individual's doctor and another non-medical member of the clinical team. However, organisations such as MIND would argue against this compulsory form of treatment, stating that the patient has the right to refuse treatment in the same way that they would have the right to refuse physical treatment; therefore they should be able to refuse psychiatric treatment (Green, 2000). Compulsory treatment should only be given in accordance with the principle of beneficence, i.e. it should be given with the client's well being in mind and not for any other purpose, such as administrative convenience or increased manageability of the patient. Moreover, the independence of the second opinion system has been questioned and conclusions drawn that the system is loaded against the individual and in favour of the RMO and the clinical team. The MHAC cited that in 87.4 per cent of the cases, second opinion doctors made no change to the treatment plan proposed by RMOs. Only 11 per cent made slight changes and just 1.6 per cent made significant changes (MHAC, 1999).

Given that the second opinion doctors' authorisation of treatment is binding, and not advisory (Fennell, 1996), the ability of individuals to resist and refuse treatment is severely limited. Whilst best practice determines the need to work collaboratively with individuals in treatment, it is debatable whether the coercive nature of the intervention or care promotes therapeutic relationships. This again compounds the individual's powerlessness in this environment and limits their ability to exercise choice and initiate action with regard to any treatment that they feel might best suit their needs.

Under Part IV of the Act, there is provision to enable urgent treatment to be administered. Circumstances under which urgent treatment can be carried out are laid down in section 62 and it must be immediately necessary to save life, which excludes treatment for a physical condition. Fennell (1996) claimed that the limits on hazardous treatments do not offer adequate protection for patients and further suggested 'statute law is proving excellent at authorising treatment without consent and at accepting coercive practice into the medical treatment' (Fennell, 1996: 232).

Personal relationships

Opportunities for self-determination will also be compromised in the individual's interpersonal relationships. It is apparent that on admission the individual will have to tolerate a number of losses which would have previously contributed to their sense of identity as a person, for example, the loss of immediate contact with family and friends, and the loss of roles associated with these relationships. While the person still continues to be a son or daughter, partner or friend, these roles are now subsumed by their position and role as 'patient', with the consequent lack of choice and ability for self-determination. The continuation of these relationships and the role that the individual has within them will now have to be negotiated with the clinical team. Visits to and from family and friends have to be planned, and, certainly in high or medium security units, have to be facilitated by escorting staff. The opportunity for the individual to receive validation as an individual and not just as a patient is therefore limited, and at best mediated, by staff presence. Ramon (1991) argued that this is a double act of devaluation, one at the beginning of the process and one at the end. The outcome of the beginning greatly affects the end.

Procedural security

Their new role as 'patient' is further compounded by the person's lack of choice in a number of areas including the basics of daily living. The need for procedural security (DoH, 2000) inevitably leads to the restriction of choice for the individual, systems operate which control the timing of, for example, getting up and going to bed, when to eat, when the individual is able to make a hot drink or smoke a cigarette. Procedural security therefore structures the day for individuals automatically and restricts the individual's capacity to exercise choice in their daily activities.

The emphasis on security has implications on empowerment. Nonetheless, the recommendations made by Read and Wallcraft (1992) as to how best to empower patients can be applied in secure settings. Whilst empowerment might be limited within such a setting, Kitchiner (1999) argued that the process of enabling could be more meaningful. It could help patients to assert control over factors that affect their life within a secure setting as individuals with rights to respect and dignity. Developing a critical awareness of the situation could facilitate a realistic plan of action (Gibson, 1991).

Privacy

Environmental, procedural, and relational security also combines to impact on an individual's loss of privacy. The communal nature of the environment means that individuals spend the majority of their time in the company of others, both staff and patients. Individuals will get access to their own rooms, but this is usually at set times and for set periods. Whilst this obviously impacts in general, it is often particularly pertinent if the ward environment is disturbed by the mental health needs of other individuals. In such situations individuals cannot easily remove themselves from the immediacy of the situation and, as a consequence, are dependent on staff to not only manage the situation but also to facilitate space for them. Given the difficulties of life in a secure environment, Bynoe (1992) advocated that for people detained against their will, they should be treated as citizens first and patients second, with fundamental standards, rights and expectations.

There is also a need to consider the apparent lack of privacy with regard to the individual's correspondence and telephone calls. Section 134 of the MHA 1983 authorises hospital managers in high security hospitals to withhold and inspect the incoming and outgoing mail of detained patients. Outgoing mail such as threatening letters, letters to victims, or dangerous objects in postal packages may also be withheld if it is believed that the communication is likely to cause distress or danger to the other person. An addressee may request in writing that communication from a patient be withheld. In other hospitals, i.e. medium secure hospitals, managers may only withhold outgoing mails if the addressee has requested it to be the case. Further guidance in exercising this power is available in the *Memorandum on MHA 1983*, paragraphs 279–287 (DHSS, 1987). It is also noted that high security hospitals reserve the right to randomly monitor the telephone calls of detained individuals. However, it is worthy of note that this right has been recently challenged (*R(N)* v. *Ashworth Special Hospital Authority & the Secretary of State for Health*, 2001). N argued that the right of the hospital to randomly monitor all telephone calls was incompatible with Article 8 of the HRA. Whilst it was held that the right to monitor telephone calls was proportional, following the challenge, telephone calls between individuals and their legal representatives will no longer be included in the monitoring process.

Sexual relationships

Mentally disordered offenders within secure hospitals also face the loss of their sexual identity and ability to engage in personal and intimate relationships. In general, it is apparent that intimate personal relationships are not encouraged within secure services. Where relationships do develop between individuals, at social functions for example, the relationship will have to be mediated through the relevant clinical teams, in order to ensure that any sexual activity is consenting. Recent social policy shifts towards single sex accommodation (DoH, 2000) will further limit an individual's ability to engage on an interpersonal basis with members of the opposite sex. The issue of relationships in secure settings raises many issues, both positive and negative, which cannot be addressed here. The paucity of debate and research into sexual relationships within secure settings, serves to stifle recognition of the right of detained individuals to engage in consensual sexual activity. Readers who wish to consider this area further may find the *Report of the Public Policy Committee Working Party*, from the Royal College of Psychiatrists (1996), a useful starting point. Whilst its focus is on sexual abuse and harassment in psychiatric settings, it provides useful guidance with regard to the development of policies covering acceptable consenting sexual activity within units, and stresses the need for patients' Individual Care Plans to be tailored to these wider policies. However, in general, it seems clear that the impact of such apparent personal disincentives for individuals detained within a secure hospital cannot be minimised, and appears to further compound their lack of ability to exercise choice.

Principles and policies for detention and treatment

It is expected that hospital managers follow policies that provide guidance on good practice and that Article 8 of the HRA is respected. The exercising of this power is subject to review by the MHAC under section 121(7).

Those who are asked to apply the provisions of the Act will be concerned not to be involved in incarcerating or administering of treatments that may not be ethical. Also to be considered is that the provisions of any order for compulsory detention must be predicated on the ethical principle of nonmaleficence, the obligation to do no harm. This is outlined by Frankena (1973) as:

1. Do no harm.
2. Prevent harm.
3. Remove harm.
4. Promote good.

These elements are arranged in rank order so that the first principle takes precedence over the second etc. Any move to restrict the autonomy of a client must adhere to these principles.

The concept of beneficence partners that of nonmaleficence, and refers to actions done for the benefit of others (Beauchamp and Childress, 2001). The rules of obligation here are clear:

1. Protect and defend the rights of others.
2. Prevent harm from occurring to others.
3. Remove conditions that will cause harm to others.
4. Help persons with disabilities.
5. Rescue persons in danger.

Although there may be confusion when trying to apply these two ethical standpoints, they do provide a framework through which we can judge the ethical justification for curtailing the freedom of the mentally disordered offender. These ethical theories oblige us to take into account the well being of the general public as well as that of the mentally disordered offender.

The application of an ethical framework will have a direct link to values. Every person has the right to feel that they are able to participate fully in society, and treatment plans and interventions should reflect this. Some basic values need to be born in mind; people with mental illness can recover and lead healthy and productive lives, even those who have offended whilst mentally ill. Also it can be argued that mentally disordered offenders have a right to appropriately funded research that will benefit them and the community. All mentally ill people should have access to a full array of high quality integrated mental health services. These values should apply to the mentally disordered offender as they should to any other person in need of mental health care.

It is clear that admission to secure hospital leads mentally disordered offenders to experience considerable loss, for example of their social role, choices and the opportunity for self-determination. Obviously the secure hospital system needs to ensure that individuals receive treatments and interventions for their acute mental health needs in a safe secure environment, where risk to staff and individuals is assessed and managed on an on-going basis. It is also important to acknowledge that for many individuals a secure ward or unit enables them to participate in support and treatment, which will promote their recovery from their acute mental health needs, and their related chaotic and traumatic life experiences. However, the way in which secure hospital provision is structured, together with the impact of the process of admission, quite clearly appears to compound disadvantage and will inevitably lead to powerlessness for individuals both in emotional and physical ways during the period of detention.

Summary

- Whilst secure services aim to promote a person's recovery from severe mental health problems, an individual may face a number of challenges to their identity as an individual, opportunities for self-determination and contact with family and friends.
- Compulsory treatment should be administered in accordance with the principle of beneficence and within the legal framework. It should only be given with the person's well being in mind and not for any other purpose.

Case study

Mr C received a four year custodial sentence for stabbing a man in a public place. The incident occurred in a restaurant and was thought to be unprovoked. At the time of sentencing, psychiatric assessments and reports were not requested. Mr C had no known history of mental health problems, although family and friends reported that he had always presented as a solitary individual, slightly eccentric and with a tendency to drink alcohol to excess at times.

Mr C originated from the South Coast, and was initially sent to his local prison. Mr C was described as an 'unremarkable prisoner', was usually quiet and caused no trouble.

However, Mr C was the victim of an attack by another prisoner, just over halfway through his sentence. Mr C sustained significant injuries from this attack and was described by Officers as withdrawn and 'depressed' following it. Mr C's behaviour appeared to deteriorate.

Officers noted that he started to express suicidal ideas and engage in self-harming behaviour, which was increasing in intensity. Mr C was moved within the prison system on a number of occasions largely as a result of perceived risk and, what was perceived as his increasingly disruptive behaviour. Psychiatrists ultimately assessed Mr C and recommended admission to secure hospital for treatment. Mr C felt that this was an inappropriate assessment and did not agree with the plans to admit him for treatment.

Recommendations were made that a transfer take place as soon as possible as professionals were aware that Mr C's day of release was in the near future and were keen to establish a transfer before this. However, negotiations with Mr C's responsible Health Authority were long and protracted. It was unclear whether ongoing funding for Mr C's treatment would be available. The Health Authority did eventually agree funding, on the day before Mr C's possible release. Mr C was transferred to a psychiatric unit in the Midlands the day before his release.

This case study demonstrates how systems can operate to compound disadvantage. Mr C was transferred to a secure psychiatric facility the day before his release. His detention within the psychiatric system is not for a given period of time, but depends on risk assessment and clinical evidence and judgement.

The question then arises as to how this will affect his engagement in treatment, and the staff's ability to work effectively with him.

Mental Health Act Commission

One important body that serves to protect the interests of individuals detained under the MHA 1983 is the Mental Health Act Commission (MHAC). Section 121 of the MHA 1983 provides for the establishment of the MHAC with the remit to carry out the functions under section 120. It therefore, on behalf of the Secretary of State, keeps under review the exercise of the powers and the discharge of duties conferred or imposed by the Act.

The MHAC is primarily concerned with the care and treatment of detained individuals. Individuals with families are able to contact the Commission for advice and support at any time during their admission. The Commission also visits all psychiatric units in the UK, during the year. Visits are either patient focussed or service focused. The Commission is also able to visit at short notice, to undertake a spot check. With regards to patient focused visits, the particular hospital has a duty to inform all patients, both individually and communally, of an impending visit and ask them whether they want to meet Commission members. Commissioners should have access to private space in order to interview patients and have the right to visit off ward areas to pursue issues that have been raised by a patient. Commissioners will also observe conditions of detention, monitor operation of the MHA 1983, implementation of the Code of Practice (COP), offer advice and guidance with regard to the Act and follow up on previous recommendations.

Protecting detainee's rights

Finally, we would like to make reference to other systems that exist to protect the rights of individuals' detained within the secure hospital system. All patients detained should be able to access independent advocacy services, either through local or national organisations, i.e. MIND, Rethink, etc. (*www.mind.org.net* and *www.rethink.org*). Such services and the workers within them are there to consult with individuals or groups of detained individuals and advocate for their perspective, rather than convey their own view or judgement. Advocates are able to attend significant meetings with individuals, i.e. ward rounds, CPA meeting, MHRTs, and can support the individual in making complaints to the relevant organisation.

Advocacy features as a central theme in the draft Mental Health Bill (DoH, 2002). Within the draft legislation, advocacy must be made available to all detained individuals and indeed the draft proposal stipulates that it would be unlawful to deny the individual a right to advocacy. The responsibilities of the advocate are clearly outlined:

1. To obtain information about the patient's treatment.
2. To inform patients of their legal rights.
3. To help patients exercise those rights by way of representation.

Summary

- Rights of detained individuals are safeguarded and promoted through legal representation, Mental Health Review Tribunals, the Mental Health Act Commission and advocacy services.
- The Human Rights Act (1998) has had an important bearing on certain aspects of the mental health system

Conclusion

Whilst ultimately promoting their recovery from mental illness, life for detained individuals within secure mental health services is restrictive and can compound disadvantage. Secure care for mentally disordered offenders can be more punitive than the criminal justice system as a prison sentence is finite whereas a detention order is based upon a multi-disciplinary assessment and can be renewed on more than one occasion. It is ironic that power ultimately lies with the clinical team, when the ethos of care should be based upon partnership, respect and empowerment. As a consequence, processes are required to protect the rights of individuals, challenge disadvantage, and the power differentials, implicit within the system.

References

Aiyegbusi, A. (2000) The experience of black mentally disordered offenders. In Chaloner, C. and Coffey, M. (Eds.) *Forensic Mental Health Nursing: Current Approaches*. London: Blackwell Science.

Beauchamp, T.L. and Childress, J.F. (2001) *Principles of Biomedical Ethics*. Oxford: Oxford University Press.

BBC Online: www.news.bbc.co.uk/1/hi/health/230179.stm 08/12/98.

Bynoe, I. (1992) *Treatment, Care and Security: Waiting for Change*. London: MIND.

Clare, A. (1998) *Understanding Psychiatric Treatment: Therapy for Serious Mental Disorder in Adults*. London: John Wiley & Sons.

Cutcliffe, J. (2001) Mass media, 'monsters' and mental health clients: the need for increased lobbying. *Journal of Psychiatric and Mental Health Nursing*. 8: 4, 315.

DoH and Home Office (1994) *Report of the Department of Health and Home Office Working Group On Psychopathic Disorder*. London: DoH.

DHSS (1983) *Mental Health Act 1983*. London: HMSO.

DHSS (1987) *Mental Health Act 1983. Memorandum on Parts I to VI, VIII and X*. London: HMSO.

DoH (1992) *Home Office. Review of Health and Social Services for Mentally Disordered Offenders and Others Requiring Similar Services*, (The Reed Report). London: HMSO.

DoH (1996) *Building Bridges*. London: HMSO.

DoH (1999) *Mental Health Act 1983: Code of Practice*. London: The Stationery Office.

DoH (1999a) *Report of the Committee of Inquiry Into the Personality Disorder Unit, Ashworth Hospital*. London: The Stationery Office.

DoH (1999b) *Effective Care Co-ordination in Mental Health Services. Modernising the Care Programme Approach. A Policy Booklet*. London: The Stationery Office.

DoH (2000) *Safety, Privacy and Dignity in Mental Health Units: Guidance on Mixed Sex Accommodation for Mental Health Services*. London: DoH.

DoH (2002) *Draft Mental Health Bill*. Cmd 5538–1. London: The Stationery Office.

DoH (2002) *Women's Mental Health: Into the Main Stream. Strategic Development of Mental Health Care for Women*. London: The Stationery Office.

Duggan, C. (1997) (Ed.) Assessing Risk in the Mentally Disordered. Supplement. *British Journal of Psychiatry*. 32: 1–3.

Fennell, P. (1996) *Treatment Without Consent*. London: Routledge.

Frankena, W. (1973) *Ethics.*(2nd edn. Englewood Cliffs NJ: Prentice Hall.

Gibson, C.H. (1991) A concept analysis of empowerment. *Journal of Advanced Nursing*. 16: 354–61.

Glover G., Leese, M. and McCrone, P. (1999) More severe mental illness is concentrated in deprived areas. *British Journal of Psychiatry*. 175: 544–8.

Green, C, (2000) Mental health care and human rights. *Mental Health Practice*. 4: 4.

Hodgins, S. and Miller-Isberner, R. (2000) *Violence, Crime and Mentally Disordered Offenders: Methods for Effective Treatment and Prevention*. London: John Wiley & Sons.

Home Office (2001) *The Human Rights Act Research Unit, Lord Chancellor's Department, www.lcd.gov.uk/hract/hramenu.htm*

Home Office and DHSS (1975) *Report of the Committee on Mentally Abnormal Offenders*. (Butler Report) Cmnd. 6244, London: HMSO.

Hotopf, M., Buchanan, A. and Churchill, R. (2000) Changing patterns in the use of the Mental Health Act 1983 in England 1984–1996. *British Journal of Psychiatry*. 176: 479–84.

Kitchiner, N. (1999) Empowerment of mentally disordered offenders within a controlled environment. In Turbuck, P., Topping-Morris, B. and Burnard, P. (Eds.) *Forensic Mental Health Nursing, Strategy and Implementation*. London: Whurr.

Lelliott, P., Audini, B. and Duuffett, R. (2001) Survey of patients from an inner-london health authority in medium secure psychiatric care. *British Journal of Psychiatry*. 178: 62–6.

Maden, A. (2001) Medium secure care and research in forensic psychiatry. *British Journal of Psychiatry*. 178: 5–6.

Mental Health Act Commission (1999) *Biennial Report 1997–99*. London: The Stationery Office.

Mullen, P. (2000) Forensic mental health. *British Journal of Psychiatry*. 176: 307–11.

Munro, E. and Rumgay, J. (2000) Role of risk assessment in reducing homicides by people with mental illness. *British Journal of Psychiatry*. 176: 116–20.

Petch, E. (2001) Risk Management in UK Mental Health Services. *Psychiatric Bulletin*. 25: 203–5.

Ramon, S. (1991) Principles and conceptual knowledge. In: Ramon, S. (Ed.) *Beyond Community Care. Normalisation and Integration Work.* London: Macmillan.

Read, J. and Wallcraft, J. (1992) *Guidelines for Empowering Users of Mental Health Services.* London: Confederation of Health Service Employees/MIND.

Robinson, D. and Kettles, A. (2000) *Forensic Nursing and Multi disciplinary Care of Mentally Disordered Offenders.* London: Jessica Kingsley Publishers.

Rose, N. (1998) Living dangerously: risk thinking and risk management in mental health care. *Mental Health Care.* 1: 8, 263–6.

Royal College of Psychiatrists (1996) *Report of the Public Policy Committee Working Party: Sexual Abuse and Harassment in Psychiatric Settings.* London: Royal College of Psychiatrists.

Taylor, P. and Gunn, J. (1999) Homicides by people with mental illness. *British Journal of Psychiatry.* 174: 9–14.

Chapter 6

Mentally Vulnerable Adults in Prison: Policy and Provision

Alice Mills

Introduction

Within the prison culture, vulnerable prisoners tend to be seen as those who are susceptible to attack from others, and are segregated for their own protection under Rule 45, or kept in vulnerable prisoner units (VPUs). These include sex offenders, police informers or 'grasses'. Yet vulnerability in prison may also be related to an individual's mental and emotional state and their ability to adjust and adapt to prison life, and as such, mentally disordered prisoners could be classed as more vulnerable than many other prisoners.

In discussing mentally disordered prisoners, it is important to define what is meant by mental disorder. It may include serious mental illness such as psychosis, common mental illness such as depression and anxiety, and personality disorder. Mental health services in the community currently tend to focus on more serious mental illness and are considered by some commentators to be psychosis-only services, although more recently pilot projects have started to develop provision for those with personality disorders.

The Prison Service's statement of purpose states that it has a duty to look after prisoners with humanity and to help them to lead law abiding and useful lives in custody and after release. This should therefore include meeting their mental and physical health needs through appropriate treatment, as well as ensuring that their mental health problems and vulnerabilities are not worsened by their imprisonment. The experience of mentally disordered prisoners, and the responsibilities of the Prison Service and NHS to care for them, is the focus of this chapter. It will firstly look at the prevalence of mental disorder, and the incidence of suicide and self-harm in prison, before discussing the need for prison health care of an equivalent standard to that of the NHS. Aspects of imprisonment and prison regimes which can exacerbate mental health problems and any associated vulnerability will also be examined, along with suitable accommodation for these prisoners, the state of prison health care and psychiatric services, and recent measures to introduce mental health in-reach teams into prisons. The particular mental health needs and experiences of different minority groups within the prison system is also considered.

The next chapter, *Mentally Vulnerable Adults in Prison: Specialist Resources and Practice*, will then focus on the provision of specialist resources, regimes and practice for dealing with the particular problems arising for prisoners with mental health problems. Risk assessment and management procedures for mentally disordered prisoners and those who are vulnerable to suicide or self-harm will also be addressed before an examination of how these prisoners might be given help to resettle back into the community.

Prevalence of mental health problems

According to a study carried out in 1997 by the Office for National Statistics (ONS) (Singleton et al., 1998), over 90 per cent of prisoners suffer from one or more of the psychiatric disorders measured (personality disorder, psychosis, neurosis, alcohol misuse and drug dependence). Of prisioners, only five per cent of males on remand, eight per cent of males sentenced, four per cent of females on remand and ten per cent of females sentenced had no such condition. The following table shows the prevalence of different psychiatric disorders within each prisoner group (hazardous drinking equates to an established pattern of alcohol consumption which confers a risk of physical or psychological harm):

Type of psychiatric disorder	Male remand %	Male sentenced %	Female %
Any personality disorder	78	64	50
Any functional psychosis	10	7	14
Any neurotic disorder	59	40	70
Hazardous drinking	58	63	38
Drug dependency	51	43	48

(Adapted from Singleton et al., 1998).

Many prisoners have more than one disorder with 54 per cent of male remand prisoners, 44 per cent of male sentenced prisoners, 61 per cent of female remand and 42 per cent of female sentenced prisoners suffering from three or more (Singleton et al., 1998). Remand prisoners clearly suffer from more, and more serious, mental health problems than sentenced ones. This is partly because the remand population contains people with severe disorders who have been remanded into custody for psychiatric reports or who have not yet been transferred to NHS care, even though they are eligible under the Mental Health Act 1983. The remand period can also be extremely stressful for prisoners, particularly due to the uncertainties surrounding legal and family issues, which may induce certain mental health problems such as depression or anxiety.

Unsurprisingly, prisoners have considerably higher rates of mental illness compared to the general population. Surveys of mental illness in the community have found that between three and seven per cent of men and one per cent of women suffer from a personality disorder (Singleton et al., 1998). Approximately 0.4 per cent of the general population could be diagnosed with a functional psychosis such as schizophrenia, mania or severe depression (Meltzer et al., 1995). Neurotic disorders are between three and five times more common among prisoners, as only 12 per cent of males and 20 per cent of females in the community suffer from them (Singleton et al., 1998; Marshall et al., 2000).

There is some evidence to suggest that levels of mental illness in the prison population have risen considerably in recent years, as earlier studies of mental disorders found significantly lower levels than the ONS research. Gunn et al. (1991) found that 38.8 per cent of sentenced population had a psychiatric diagnosis, and a level of 63 per cent was found for the remand population a few years later (Brooke et al., 1996). The increase may represent a genuine growth in the number of people admitted to prison with some sort of mental disorder, possibly as a result of under-resourced community care policies (Coggan and Walker, 1982; Bowden, 1990; Grounds 1990; Richer, 1990), but it might also be explained by the methodology used. Gunn et al. (1991) and Brooke et al. (1996) used clinical interviews carried out by psychiatrists, whereas the ONS study used lay interviews, with only a small proportion of the sample being assessed by an additional clinical interview. Furthermore, the studies used slightly different diagnostic systems, and as such they may not be directly comparable. The fact that mental disorder 'remains there at all to be diagnosed at these levels' should be the principal concern (Peay, 2002) and undoubtedly means that the Prison Service needs to deliver some form of mental healthcare provision for these prisoners, even though many of them should not be in prison at all.

Incidence of suicide or self-harm

Concern has recently been demonstrated about the high number of suicides and incidents of self-harm carried out by prisoners. In the first half of 2003, 7,692 incidents of self-harm were recorded, with 52.8 per cent of these taking place within male prisons and 45.9 in female prisons (the remaining 1.3 per cent of incidents occurred in the care of court escort contractors). This indicates a rise of 30 per cent in comparison to the same period in 2002, although this may be partly associated with improvements in the method of reporting self-harm (Self-Harm Report 2003, published on Prison Service Quantum website). The number of suicides has also risen from 47 in 1993 to 94 in 2003, with 85 per cent taking place in male prisons and 15 per cent in female establishments in 2003 (HM Prison Service, 2001a; Howard League, 2004).

The history of policy on mental health care in prison and the demand for equivalence

One of the most significant reports on mentally disordered offenders and their care in prison was the Reed Report, (DoH/Home Office, 1992), which reaffirmed government policy that mentally disordered offenders should receive care and treatment from social and health services rather than from the criminal justice system. It aimed to review the 'level and range of provision that needs to be in place to enable mentally disordered offenders and similar patients to receive care and treatment in the most suitable location' (DoH/Home Office, 1992). The report recommended that mentally disordered offenders who fall under the confines of the Mental Health Act 1983 should be diverted out of the criminal justice system as soon as possible, either through court diversion schemes, or transfer from prison. Additionally, it called for a clear statement of policy on the care and treatment of prisoners with mental healthcare needs and strongly endorsed the decision of an Efficiency Scrutiny of the then Prison Medical Service in 1990 (which became the Heath Care Service for Prisoners) that healthcare services should be contracted into prisons, mainly from the NHS. This was to be done initially for remand prisoners, in order to offer better quality care for mentally disordered offenders, and ensure better continuity of care on release or transfer to hospital.

Many commentators have supported this idea that prison healthcare services should be provided by the NHS, as it would ensure equivalence of prison healthcare with that of the general population (King and Morgan, 1980, Coggan and Walker 1982; Gostin and Staunton 1985; Sim 1990; Gunn et al., 1991; Grounds, 1994; Reed and Lyne, 1997). Although Prison Health Care Standards state that prisoners have 'access to the same range and quality of services as the general public receives from the National Health Service (HM Prison Service, 2002a: Section 22), in 1997 only 65 establish-ments were able to comply with these standards, with the remainder reporting difficulties because of resource constraints (Directorate of Health Care, 1998). In a report on prison healthcare, *Patient or Prisoner*, Her Majesty's Chief Inspector of Prisons (HMCIP) (HMCIP, 1996) suggested that there was a particularly urgent need for improved assessment and care of mentally disordered prisoners who do not meet the criteria of the Mental Health Act 1983, and he proposed that the NHS take responsibility for the delivery of all prison healthcare. Prison Service needs would therefore be included in all resource allocation and prisoners should receive the same standard of healthcare as those in the community. Such an arrangement would also mean better continuity of treatment, appropriate monitoring and evaluation, staff trained to work in either the Prison Service or the NHS, and a common commitment to standards (HMCIP, 1996).

In 1999, a joint executive working group was set up between the Prison Service and the National Health Service to consider these proposals. Their report recognised that there were variations in effectiveness and quality of working with the NHS, with few formal, systematic links with local health authorities (Joint Prison Service and National Health Service Executive Working Group, 1999). However, they rejected the idea that responsibility for all prison healthcare should move to the NHS on the grounds that healthcare staff within prisons might become marginalised due to management and cultural differences, and that neither of the two services could provide healthcare for prisoners without the expertise of the other. The group recommended instead that a formal partnership be established between the NHS and the Prison Service, whereby the Prison Service remained responsible for primary care provision, and the NHS for secondary care, community mental health, and visiting NHS specialist support. Health authorities or Primary Care Trusts (PCTs) and prison governors became jointly responsible for planning and commissioning services based on health needs assessments, and it was thought that these measures would ensure the desired equivalence of care, as well as improving continuity of treatment on entry to and exit from prison, and reducing the isolation of clinical staff.

In relation to mental health, the report recognised that many of the more specialist services such as occupational therapy, counselling and community mental health teams were still lacking in prison, with three-quarters of the 38 prisons sampled in their study having no community support at all. It therefore recommended that the care of mentally ill prisoners should develop in line with NHS mental health policy, with special attention paid to the better identification of mental health needs at reception, and the development of community mental health outreach work on prison wings.

In order to implement these proposals, a Prison Health Policy Unit and Task Force were established, replacing the Directorate of Health Care, to develop prison healthcare policy, provide support and advisory services, and to help to implement change by working with prisons and the NHS. Both are located in the DoH, a position which Grounds (2000) sees as symbolically important, as their perspective should be health service rather than Prison Service based.

The idea of a partnership with the NHS was generally well received, although concerns were raised that some fundamental points of conflict might arise owing to differing views about the nature of regimes and potential clashes between notions of care and treatment on one hand, and the need for security and control on the other (Grounds, 2000). Furthermore, maintaining Prison Service responsibility for primary care has meant that it has not kept up with developments in the NHS (Keavney, 2001a). Some PCTs have also been reluctant to carry out prison health needs assessments to identify appropriate services and inform the necessary contracts between the prison and the NHS (HMCIP 1996; Joint Prison Service and National Health Service Executive Working Group, 1999; HM Prison Service, 2001b). Although every prison was required to have carried out a needs assessment by March 2001 (Harvey, 2001), it is thought that few prisons had done so (McGauran, 2001), and some trusts are still reluctant to engage fully with prisons in their area possibly because they recognise the level of need and demand (HMCIP, 2004).

In April 2003, however, the NHS took over the running of all prison healthcare services in England, a move which is more likely to ensure equivalence of care than any of the previous measures. NHS healthcare standards will now apply to services in prison, and an extra £46 million per year will be invested in prison healthcare by 2005–6 to be targeted at improving prison mental healthcare services and primary care (DoH, 2003; *The Guardian*, 30 September 2002). Although prison healthcare is showing noticeable and much needed improvement as well as movement towards equivalence with healthcare in the community (HMCIP, 2004), little substantial change is likely to be evident until April 2006 when full commissioning responsibility for healthcare services will be devolved to PCTs. This move will only be effective if funding is sufficient and PCTs are competent enough to supply services to prisons (Keavney, 2003). In the meantime, the majority of funding for prison health will be transferred back to the Prison Service as per current arrangements, and the proposed changes are being piloted in a number of volunteer prisons (Prison Health, 2003).

Effects of prison regime on those with such vulnerabilities

Although imprisonment may present a chance to improve prisoners' health by ensuring that they have full access to health services, mentally ill prisoners face a number of difficulties which can create or aggravate their health problems and vulnerability. The World Health Organisation (WHO) (1998) has named overcrowding, dirty and depressing environments, poor food, and inadequate medical care as factors which can have a debilitating effect on mental health (see also Penal Affairs Consortium (PAC) 1998; Woolf, 1999). Certainly prisoners may be less able to access appropriate treatment for their mental health problems because of pressures placed on services and resources by the rapidly rising prison population and the consequent overcrowding, which may also hamper staff efforts to care for individual prisoners (Levenson, 2002).

The so-called 'pains of imprisonment' (Sykes, 1958), such as the deprivation of liberty, goods, and services and security, can affect mental health and any associated vulnerability. Being locked up in a cell for long periods of time can considerably increase anxieties and depression, and a certain amount of strength may be needed to survive the boredom of prison life. Imprisonment may leave prisoners isolated from family and friends, worsening feelings of hopelessness, lowering self-esteem (Toch and Adams, 1989; Liebling, 1992), and possibly making prisoners even more vulnerable as they are left without sources of significant support. Living in close proximity to other prisoners may also make prisoners agitated or depressed, particularly if they are already fearful of bullying or victimisation (Mills, 2003). These pains are also likely to be exacerbated by overcrowding which can lead to less opportunities to participate in constructive activity or maintain contact with families through visits and telephone calls, and may increase psychological strain and lead to nervous disorders (Geary, 1980).

Yet in turn, mental health problems can affect the degree to which prisoners can ease the pains of imprisonment by engaging in constructive activity. The ONS study found that prisoners with significant neurotic symptoms, psychosis or drug dependency were more likely than others to report spending 19 or more hours a day in their cells (Singleton et al., 1998). This may be because of the medical treatment they are receiving. Those who are on strong medication may be unable to participate in work or education because of side effects or feeling 'doped up', which may worsen their sense of boredom and isolation (Mills, 2003).

Mental disorder has traditionally been an indicator of vulnerability to suicide and self-harm. Several studies have mentioned the preponderance of mental illness or psychiatric contact among those who commit suicide or self-harm (Lloyd, 1990; Liebling, 1992, 1999; HMCIP, 1999; HM Prison Service, 2001a), with many agreeing that about a third of prisoners who kill themselves were in receipt of psychiatric treatment (Lloyd, 1990). However, it should be noted that the proportion of people with experience of psychiatric treatment is lower among those who commit suicide in prison than among those who commit suicide in the community (Backett, 1987; Liebling, 1992; HMCIP, 1999). As over 90 per cent of the prison population are thought to have some sort of mental disorder, it does not adequately distinguish those who are vulnerable to suicide from the rest of the prison population. There is no evidence to suggest that the high level of psychiatric disorder amongst people who commit suicide in prison is any different from that found in the general prison population. Furthermore, many studies rely on psychiatric contact as a measure of mental disorder, which gives no indication of the actual mental state of the prisoner just before the suicide, but may refer to psychiatric problems occurring some years previously. Furthermore, opportunities for such contact may differ for a variety of reasons (Lloyd, 1990).

There is clearly then a need to examine other factors in attempting to explain vulnerability to suicide. The focus of prison suicide studies has therefore shifted from personal characteristics of vulnerable prisoners to a consideration of those factors within the prison regime, which may exacerbate individual vulnerability to suicidal behaviour (Liebling, 1992). Suicide has been seen as a response to difficulties in coping with prison life. Such difficulties arise from an interaction between internal factors such as mental health problems which may affect a prisoner's ability to cope, and environmental pressures, such as lack of activity or contact with family and friends, or victimisation by other prisoners (Toch and Adams, 1989; Liebling, 1992; Seymour, 1992; Toch, 1992, 1993; Corcoran, 1994; Drummer, 1996; Mills, 2003). Liebling (1992) found that prisoners who were at risk of suicide or self-harm were those who were more likely to have little or no contact with the outside, were more likely to spend most of the time locked up in the cells and were more likely to have problems with other prisoners. Yet they were less likely to be able to generate any solution to their predicament, for example by occupying themselves constructively in their cells, and often had a history of affective, psychological problems such as depression and substance abuse (see also HMCIP, 1990; 1999; Liebling and Krarup, 1993; Liebling, 1999; Sherratt, 1993; Howard League, 1999). This may explain the high risk of suicide on remand and in the early period of custody because prisoners may not have had the chance to develop the skills and strength necessary to cope with their imprisonment. The shock of incarceration and withdrawal from substances may be exacerbated by poor conditions and overcrowding in remand centres and local prisons.

In order to reduce this vulnerability and promote positive mental health, the Chief Inspector of Prisons has suggested that there is a need for healthy prisons (HMCIP, 1999). Within such 'healthy prisons', the weakest prisoners should feel safe, all prisoners should be treated with respect and be busily occupied, and given the opportunity to improve themselves, as well as being able to strengthen links with their families and prepare for release. All prisons should have already developed anti-bullying strategies and most have peer support schemes, such as the Listeners (specially selected prisoners who are trained by the Samaritans to befriend prisoners in distress), to promote prisoner well being and confidence.

Issues of gender, ethnicity and nationality

Certain groups within the criminal justice system may be disadvantaged in terms of access to services or provisions which might improve their mental health, despite the fact that they may suffer from considerably more mental health problems.

As can be seen from the earlier table, female prisoners are more likely than males to suffer from certain kinds of psychiatric disorder, particularly psychosis and neurotic disorders. In 1997, 40 per cent of women reported receiving help or treatment for a mental or emotional problem in the 12 months before imprisonment, double the proportion of men (Singleton et al., 1998). Rates of self-harm and suicide tend to be higher in women's prisons as women tend to react differently to imprisonment and are more likely to turn any violence in on themselves (NACRO, 1993). Attention has recently been drawn to the plight of vulnerable female prisoners, because women, who make up only six per cent of the prison population, made up 15 per cent of the suicides in prison in 2003. Six women committed suicide at one establishment between August 2002 and August 2003, leading to an independent investigation by the Prisons and Probation Ombudsman to establish the circumstances surrounding one of these deaths and what more could be done to prevent suicides in prison. Many commentators have argued that numbers of women simply should not be in prison at all due to their vulnerability, and that appropriate community provision, particularly in relation to mental health and drug treatment, should be increased and court diversion schemes prioritised (Carlen, 1990; Edgar and Rickford, 2003).

Female prisoners are currently held in only 19 prisons which are not evenly geographically spread. For example, there is no women's prison in Wales, and only one maximum security establishment, at Durham. This can make visits and the maintenance of family ties very difficult, a problem which may be particularly acute for women with children, who are likely to have been their children's primary carer. A Home Office study in 1997 found that only half of the women prisoners who lived with or had contact with their children prior to their imprisonment had received a visit from them whilst in prison (Home Office, 1997). Such lack of contact with loved ones may increase women's sense of isolation, exacerbate any mental health problems, and leave them at an enhanced risk of suicide and self-harm. These difficulties are likely to be worse for the 70 per cent of foreign national female prisoners who have children (Green, 1991), who may be imprisoned for many years having only made short-term arrangements for the care of their children; something which is likely to lead to considerable anxiety and distress. Women may also be located a substantial distance away from community mental health services that they may have previously used, and psychiatric staff may be reluctant to undertake long journeys to see them or consult with other staff about their care, leading to delays in assessment, transfer and appropriate care.

People from ethnic minorities are already over represented in the prison population, but they also make up a higher proportion of those transferred to hospital under section 47 of the Mental Health Act 1983 (Grounds, 1990). There is little agreement as to why this might be the case. It may be because they are more likely to be mentally disordered, particularly young African Caribbean males who are more likely to suffer from psychotic illness (Social Exclusion Unit (SEU), 2002), or because they are more likely to be diagnosed as such, as their behaviour is more likely to be taken as a sign of mental illness. A diagnosis of schizophrenia is often arrived at among black patients even in the absence of 'core symptoms' which are considered necessary for a similar diagnosis in white patients (Sashidaran, 1989), and the over-representation of African-Caribbean men in psychiatric treatment may therefore have arisen because of cultural misunderstanding, misdiagnosis and a readiness to use medication (Bhui, 1999). Due to their perceived danger-ousness, black people may be less likely to be diagnosed with a personality disorder because they are 'untreatable', and they may be more likely to be diagnosed with a psychotic illness instead as this enables medication and other measures to be used to control them (Bhui, 1999). A high level of serious mental illness among black and Asian prisoners might be expected to make them more vulnerable to suicide and self-harm, but statistics for the years 1996–2002 suggest that the number of self-inflicted deaths amongst this group is proportionately lower, as they make up 20 per cent of the prison population, but only nine per cent of the number of self-inflicted deaths (Joint Committee on Human Rights, 2004).

Black offenders may have less chance of being diverted out of the criminal justice system at an earlier stage. A study of Magistrates' court cases where psychiatric reports on defendants were requested, found that white defend-ants were more likely to be granted bail, and lengths of custodial remands were longer for black defendants, possibly because of magistrates being affected by a heightened perception of their dangerousness (NACRO et al., 1990; see also Bhui, 1999). Black and ethnic minority prisoners may also have less access to services within the prison system. In their study of Grendon, a prison which offers a therapeutic regime (see Chapter 7, *Mentally Vulnerable Adults in Prison: Specialist Resources and Practice*, for a more detailed discussion of this). Genders and Player (1995) found that few black and ethnic minority prisoners were located there. This was attributed to the way that they were stereotyped by prison staff, with Asian prisoners thought to have inadequate English to engage with 'talking therapies' and black prisoners viewed as intrinsically volatile and unamenable to social control, or simply being uninterested in seeking such help.

The growing number of foreign national prisoners may also face specific difficulties in relation to their own mental health and accessing appropriate services. They currently make up 12 per cent of the prison population and one in four women prisoners (HMCIP, 2004). Although in general little is known about their mental health and associated vulnerability, there is some evidence to suggest that their general mental health needs may be greater because of the strains that they face being in a foreign country and criminal justice system, and they may be at a higher risk of suffering conditions such as Post Traumatic Stress Disorder, because of experiences of torture, persecution and abuse in their home countries before they arrived in Britain (Bhui, 2004). They are likely to feel more isolated than other prisoners due to a lack of visits from family members and the expense of phone calls, and may be unable to alleviate any boredom as they may have little or no access to reading materials in their own language or be unable to participate in other activities owing to language difficulties, possibly leaving them at greater risk of suicide or self-harm. Furthermore, foreign nationals may be unable to communicate with health care staff and other prisoners. Yet since 1994 every Prison Service establishment and immigration centre has been connected to Language Line, a telephone interpreter service which connects the caller to an interpreter in the language of their choice. This can enable staff to talk to foreign national prisoners, but is currently woefully under-used. Staff and prisoners are not always aware of its existence and prisoners may be intimidated by a perceived connection with the prison authorities. Use of Language Line is also seen as expensive and staff may require permission from governors or wing managers to use it, even though it may actually reduce costs as it decreases the need for expensive face-to-face interpretation (Bhui, 2004).

Accommodating prisoners with mental health problems

In order to alleviate the distress of prisoners with mental health problems and those at risk of suicide or self-harm, there is a need to make sure that they are placed in appropriate accommodation whilst in prison. Many prisoners with severe mental health problems or who are identified as being at risk of suicide will be accommodated in prison healthcare centres, a practice which the Chief Inspector of Prisons (HMCIP, 2001: 67) called 'a national disgrace', as they rarely provide adequate levels of support and stimulation (HMCIP, 2004), often due to the lack of opportunities to participate in constructive activities such as work or education. Recently it has been argued that shared accommodation on normal prison wings is more appropriate for this group of prisoners as it allows them to participate in the prison regime and receive support from staff and other prisoners (Lloyd, 1990; HM Prison Service, 1997; HMCIP, 1999; Joint Prison Service and National Health Service Executive Working Group, 1999; Medlicott, 1999; DoH et al., 2001), although here they may encounter difficulties with other prisoners and be at risk of victimisation owing to their vulnerability (Gunn et al., 1991).

In the past strip (or 'special') cells have been used to accommodate prisoners for short periods of time if they were deemed to be in serious danger of harming themselves or others, damaging property or causing a disturbance (Prison Service Order 1600), or if transfer to the NHS was not possible or delayed (Coid et al., 2003). Yet those placed in such cells could be among the most vulnerable in the system as Coid et al. (2003) found that prisoners who had been put there had extensive experience of previous psychiatric treatment, and they were more likely to be screened positively for 'probable psychosis' and to report previous suicide attempts and self-harm.

The use of strip cells, particularly for suicidal prisoners, has been widely criticised. They have no furniture, decoration or clothing and may have no natural light, exposing prisoners to what is essentially sensory deprivation (Sherratt, 1993). They are likely to be seen as a punitive, rather than a therapeutic measure, and this may deter prisoners from asking for help for fear of being placed there (Liebling, 1992; 1999; Liebling and Krarup, 1993), thus increasing the risk of them committing self-destructive acts. Depriving prisoners of human contact may actually serve to intensify a sense of hopelessness, lower their self-esteem and increase suicidal ideas rather than relieve distress (Liebling, 1992; 1999; Dooley, 1994; Gunn, 1998 cited in HMCIP, 1999). In his thematic review of suicide and self-harm, the then Chief Inspector of Prisons stated that no one who is actively suicidal should be left on their own, and recommended that prisoners at risk of suicide should be placed in as normal an environment as possible and preferably in shared accommodation (HMCIP, 1999; see also Lloyd, 1990; Medlicott , 1999). Following this, the Prison Service announced that the use of strip cells for suicidal prisoners would be eliminated by April 2000, as this practice was likely to be challenged under Article 3 of the Human Rights Act 1998 which enshrines the European Convention of Human Rights into UK law, and protects the right to freedom from torture or inhuman or degrading treatment or punishment (Levenson, 2000; Cheney et al., 2001). Suicide prevention policy now states that at risk prisoners should be allocated to shared accommodation where possible and that active supportive contact should be made rather than just observation. It also introduced safe cells; that is, cells that are free of ligature points and contain indestructible furniture (Safer Custody Group, 2000; HM Prison Service, 2002b), which should be located in areas such as healthcare centres, and induction and detoxification units in high risk prisons. Although these may physically prevent suicide and self-harm, and comply with the Human Rights Act, the case of a prisoner suicide in one Young Offender's Institution (The Guardian, 13 October 2002) has shown that these may not always be available. They may also be used as an excuse not to maintain active, supportive contact, leaving prisoners isolated from others and exacerbating feelings of hopelessness and any consequent risk of suicide (Dooley, 1994). Suitable accommodation is needed, which meets the needs of these prisoners and addresses their difficulties of coping with prison life, rather than making them more vulnerable, and this might include wing-based initiatives, such as the facilities for prisoners with special needs described in the next chapter.

Prisoners with mental health problems or coping difficulties may also be vulnerable to violent outbursts as a result of their own frustrations (Corcoran, 1994). Mentally disordered prisoners tend to have a higher rate of disciplinary infractions than other prisoners, and they are more likely to be placed in disciplinary segregation because of such behaviour (Health Advisory Committee for the Prison Service (HAC), 1997), and may also be moved around the prison system despite their need for specialist healthcare (HMCIP, 2004). Yet segregation may serve to worsen the pressures of prison life and intensify mental health problems as well as the risk of suicide or self-harm due to the lack of constructive activity and human contact (Hagel-Seymour, 1982; Adams, 1986; Gunn et al., 1991; Hodgins and Côté, 1991; Miller, 1994). The segregation of prisoners with a history of mental illness without a full mental state assessment and a care plan can constitute a breach of Article 3 of the European Convention of Human Rights (see above) (Safer Custody News, 2002).

Prison health care and psychiatric services

For the many prisoners with mental health problems who do not fall within the provisions of the Mental Health Act 1983, and thus do not meet the criteria for transfer to NHS care (see below), there is a need to ensure that they have access to suitable mental healthcare in prison. Yet before any treatment can be administered to them, they have to be assessed as suffering from some form of mental disorder. An initial assessment to identify physical and mental health needs as well as risk of suicide or self-harm should be carried out by a healthcare worker on reception into prison, to be followed up by a physical and mental health assessment by a doctor within 24 hours (HM Prison Service, 2002a). Such assessments have been the subject of much criticism, as they may not take place in private, prisoners may not feel free to tell staff of any problems and they may be rushed, particularly in busy local

prisons, making effective screening and medical examination virtually impossible (Reed and Lyne, 1997; Joint Prison Service and National Health Service
Executive Working Group, 1999). Additionally, little information may be
passed on from other agencies regarding previous psychiatric treatment (HAC,
1997). A study by Birmingham et al. (1996) found that 75 per cent of mental
disorder is not recognised at reception, and although mental health problems
may be picked up later on the wings by other members of staff, by this time the
prisoner may have suffered unnecessarily through a lack of care. As a result of
these criticisms, improved reception screening procedures are currently being
piloted in ten prisons. These consist of 15 questions, with the initial part of the
screening identifying those who need further assessment, management or
treatment. A more in-depth assessment should then take place within 24–48
hours where needed. An initial evaluation of these procedures has shown that
they successfully identified 91 per cent of those withdrawing from substances,
51 per cent with some mental illness and 86 per cent with severe mental illness
(HM Prison Service, 2001a), a clear improvement on previous screening tools,
and this new system is currently being introduced into all local prisons. The
Joint Prison/Probation Offender Assessment System (OASys), which identifies
core needs and risks and is used when preparing pre-sentence reports, can also
flag up mental disorder and vulnerability to suicide and self-harm. If mental
disorder is identified, offenders should then be referred by a probation officer
for a more thorough mental health assessment. Unfortunately, however, there
are currently no links between OASys and the new reception screening
procedures, despite their potential use in picking up on low level indications of
mental disorder at an early stage and in ensuring that appropriate care plans
can be developed as soon as possible.

As there has been an emphasis on improving the transfer of the seriously
mentally ill into NHS care, there has been a neglect of those with less serious
problems, and psychiatric services in many prisons have been rather limited.
In their study of prisoners identified with 'probable psychosis', Melzer et al.
(2002) found that only 53 per cent reported having any treatment for a
mental, drug abuse or emotional problem within the last year, with only a
quarter having appointments with psychiatric professionals; the ONS study
found that approximately one in seven prisoners were refused help such as
medication, counselling or a psychiatrist session during their imprisonment
(Singleton et al., 1998). In the community, those with serious mental illness
would have the possibility of contact with a number of support services such
as a consultant psychiatrist, community psychiatric nurse and day centres
(Staite, 1995). However, in their review of 19 prison inspections, Reed and
Lyne (1997) noted that none of the prisons had arrangements for all mentally
disordered inpatients to be under the care of a consultant psychiatrist and
none had a full multi-disciplinary mental health team.

Mentally disordered prisoners may also suffer from inadequate care owing to a lack of appropriately trained staff. They may be under the care of a prison doctor and nurses with little, if any, training in psychiatry (HAC, 1997; Keavney, 2001b), and staff may be reliant on consultations and decisions from visiting psychiatrists, who may be inappropriate for the job due to lack of forensic experience or ability to secure NHS beds (Sim, 1990; Gunn et al., 1991; HMCIP, 1996). The Prison Service has been affected by the general shortage of available mental health nurses (Directorate of Health Care, 1999). In 1998, only 20 per cent of nursing staff were Registered Mental Health Nurses, when the Service requires 60 per cent to be qualified in mental health nursing (Directorate of Health Care, 1999).

Prison is clearly not the most suitable place to offer psychiatric treatment. Treating schizophrenia in the community, for example, involves examining the patient's environment, social relationships, occupational activities and daycare, yet it may not be possible to change the environment or activities in a prison setting (Grounds, 1990). Mental healthcare in prison can also rely heavily on medication (Stevens, 1998). About one fifth of the men and half of the women prisoners in the ONS study were taking some form of medication acting on the central nervous system (Singleton et al., 1998). Such medication may alleviate the symptoms of mental disorder, but may have significant side effects (Coggan and Walker, 1982), and prescribed drugs can be used as currency within prison. Prisoners may be bullied for their medication, thus enhancing their vulnerability to victimisation. Some prisons may choose not to prescribe certain drugs such as benzodiazepines, even if prisoners enter prison with such a prescription (Reed and Lyne, 1997). This is clearly not healthcare equivalent with the NHS, prisons may even prescribe cheaper rather than the most appropriate drugs, which could have adverse effects on prisoners' health (Keavney, 2001b).

Mental health in-reach services

Recent policy developments have, however, suggested that mental healthcare in prison is likely to improve considerably in the next three to five years. In November 2001, proposals for the development of improved mental health services for prisoners in line with the National Service Framework for Mental Health and the NHS plan were announced (DoH et al., 2001). These affirmed the need to make sure that prisoners have access to the correct range of services to NHS standards, to improve arrangements for transferring seriously ill prisoners to NHS care, and to reduce the number of prisoners located in prison healthcare centres and the average length of time they spend there (DoH et al., 2001).

Perhaps most significantly, teams of mental health professionals, similar to Community Mental Health Teams, funded by local PCTs, are now expected to go onto prison wings and provide specialised services to prisoners in the same way as they do to patients in the community, in order to support them outside of the healthcare centre (DoH et al., 2001). These teams should involve a range of specialists including community psychiatric nurses, occupational therapists, and psychologists to offer help and advice to patients. This approach is being piloted in 22 prisons, and should be expanded by 2003/4, to the 70 prisons considered to have the greatest mental health need (DoH et al., 2001; HM Prison Service website, 6 March 2002). It is expected to benefit the approximately 5,000 prisoners with severe mental health problems who are in need of comprehensive mental health treatment (DoH, 2000). The Prison Service has allocated £60 million to implement such measures (HM Prison Service, 2001b), and the NHS plan has allowed for 300 extra mental health staff over three years to support the implementation of these Mental Health In-reach teams (DoH, 2000). These services are already starting to have an impact in terms of ensuring that those with serious mental disorder are better managed on prison wings, and reducing the number of inpatient beds, whilst increasing the number of daycare places available to support those who find it difficult to cope on normal location (see below) (HMCIP, 2004).

Nevertheless, it has been recognised that there are likely to be problems introducing such provision in terms of modifying existing accommodation and training staff (DoH et al., 2001). In particular, concern has been raised that it will be difficult to find so many new mental health staff to work in prisons, particularly as mental health nurses are in short supply within the community (Shooter, 2001). According to the Prison Reform Trust (2003), in 2003 there were only 42 functioning in-reach teams within the prison system, with only 155 staff, which equates to one member of staff for every 322 prisoners suffering from mental disorders. Prison regimes may also need modernising to accommodate caring social and clinical health programmes to ensure not only that appropriate care is offered, but also that appropriate professional staff can be recruited and retained (Keavney, 2003). Furthermore, the in-reach services may be limited to those with severe mental disorders, meaning that those with less serious mental health problems will not benefit from such measures, although the importance of anti-bullying policies and availability of emotional support, particularly through the Listener schemes, in promoting good mental health has been recognised (DoH et al., 2001). Finally, Peay (2002) has criticised the proposals, seeing the only humane option as transferring mentally disordered prisoners to NHS care, where they can receive compulsory treatment and avoid victimisation and self-harm; many prisoners, however, do not meet the criteria for NHS services as they do not suffer from serious mental illness.

Daycare

Daycare services can offer a variety of activities and therapies for prisoners who might otherwise be unable to participate in work or education. These could entail sessions to develop life and practical skills including activities such as washing and preparing food (DoH et al., 2001), and creative and art therapy which allows prisoners to express their feelings when they may not have the social skills to discuss them. The Daycare unit at HMP Cardiff is one example of how daycare can operate in prisons. It is staffed by a full-time occupational therapist and two full-time nurses, and provides a range of therapeutic groups and individual support sessions based on the needs of prisoners. These aim to improve prisoners' cognitive and functional skills, and include subjects such as anger management, relaxation training and drug and alcohol awareness (Thurston et al., 2001). A study of prisoners with special needs at this establishment, many of whom had mental health problems, found that over half of those who had attended daycare found it beneficial because it gave them an opportunity to discuss their problems and enter a more relaxed environment. Others were not always clear about its purpose and this sometimes led to it being described as 'boring' or 'pointless' (Mills, 2003). Occupational therapy can certainly improve a person's emotional resilience (WHO, 1998), and is suitable not only for the mentally disordered, but also those with learning difficulties and those who find it difficult to cope with prison life (HMCIP, 2000a). However, such facilities are generally under-developed within the prison system and the expansion proposed as part of mental health in-reach services may be hampered by difficulties recruiting occupational therapists, particularly as the field of forensic occupational therapy is small with few appropriate training places (Mills, 2002).

Services for 'dual diagnosis' prisoners

As well as suffering from high levels of mental disorder, a large proportion of the prison population has misused one or both of drugs and alcohol before entering prison (see table on page 86). The ONS figures suggest that many prisoners could be said to have a 'dual diagnosis'; that is, they have co-existing mental health and substance misuse problems. Substance misuse and mental health problems may exacerbate each other and as those with a mental illness may use drugs or alcohol to alleviate the symptoms of their mental health problems (Harrison and Abou Saleh, 2002; Hussein Rassool, 2003; Williams, 2002), and substance misuse may induce mental health problems, a sustained period of abstinence may be required to avoid the dangers of misdiagnosis, particularly as withdrawal from substances may also produce a wide range of psychiatric symptoms (Williams, 2002). Services for this group of prisoners can be limited as neither mental healthcare nor drug or alcohol treatment services may be willing to take responsibility for them. Prisoners may not be able to access drug treatment due to mental health problems, and may be rejected from mental health services because of their substance misuse. The Royal College of Psychiatrists has expressed concern that prison drugs and healthcare policies will develop separately when there is a need for a more 'integrated' model to provide effective services for dual diagnosis prisoners (HMCIP, 2000b; Williams, 2002). The development of new mental health in-reach services should now take account of and link in with established detoxification and drug treatment programmes (DoH et al., 2001), which may go some way towards ensuring that appropriate provision is established for this group of prisoners.

Summary of main points

Clearly then, the prevalence of mental disorder is considerably higher in prison than in the community, and there is also a high incidence of suicide and self-harm amongst prisoners. Mental health problems may not be identified on reception into prison and this, along with poorly trained staff and limited psychiatric services, has meant that many prisoners have not received appropriate care and treatment. However, now that the NHS has full responsibility for prison healthcare, and mental health in-reach services have been introduced into prisons, mental health provision may finally improve and reach an equivalent standard to that provided in the community, although significant changes are unlikely to occur if the appropriate financial support, staffing and expertise are not provided.

Various aspects of the prison regime can create or exacerbate mental health problems and vulnerability to suicide or self-harm, particularly if mentally vulnerable prisoners are placed in locations such as strip cells or segregation, which can heighten their distress. Mental health in-reach services have started to reduce the number of prisoners using in-patient beds by supporting and treating those with serious mental illnesses on prison wings, where they can also have contact with others and the opportunity to participate in constructive activities.

Some groups of prisoners are not only more likely to be diagnosed with certain disorders, but are also often less able to access suitable support to help to ameliorate their distress. Women and foreign nationals are kept further away from their families and services that they may have previously used, and due to perceptions of dangerousness and cultural stereotypes, black and ethnic minority prisoners are less likely to be diverted from the criminal justice system or to receive specialist help during their imprisonment.

References

Adams, K. (1986) The disciplinary experiences of mentally disordered inmates. *Criminal Justice and Behaviour.* 13: 297–316.

Backett, S.A. (1987) Suicide in Scottish prisons. *British Journal of Psychiatry.* 151: 218–221.

Bhui, H.S. (1999) Race, racism and risk assessment: linking theory to practice with black mentally disordered offenders. *Probation Journal.* 46: 3, 171–81.

Bhui, H.S. (2004) *Developing Effective Practice with Foreign National Prisoners.* London: Prison Reform Trust.

Birmingham, L., Mason, D. and Grubin, D. (1996) The prevalence of mental disorder in remand prisoners. *British Medical Journal.* 313: 1521–4.

Bowden, P. (1990) Scene from here. *Prison Service Journal, Winter.* 57.

Brooke, D., Taylor, C., Gunn, J. and Maden, A. (1996) Point prevalence of mental disorder in unconvicted male prisoners in England and Wales. *British Medical Journal.* 313: 1524–7.

Carlen, P. (1990) *Alternatives to Women's Imprisonment.* Buckingham: Open University Press.

Cheney, D., Dickson, L., Skilbeck, R. and Uglow, S. (with Fitzpatrick, J.) (2001) *Criminal Justice and the Human Rights Act 1998*, 2nd edn. Bristol: Jordans.

Coggan, G. and Walker, M. (1982) *Frightened for my Life: An Account of Deaths in British Prisons.* Glasgow: Fontana.

Coid, J., Petruckevitch, A., Bebbington, P., Jenkins, R., Brugha, T., Lewis, G., Farrell, M. and Singleton, N. (2003) Psychiatric morbidity in prisoners and solitary cellular confinement, II: special ('strip') cells. *Journal of Forensic Psychiatry and Psychology.* 14: 2, 320–40.

Corcoran, K. (1994) Violence and the mentally ill in prisons. In Stanko, E. (Ed.) *Perspectives on Violence.* London: Quartet Books.

DoH (2000) *The NHS Plan: A Plan for Investment, A Plan for Reform.* London: The Stationery Office.

DoH (2003) *National Partnership Agreement on the Transfer of Responsibility for Prison Health from the Home Office to the DoH.* London: DoH.

DoH/Home Office (1992) *Review of Health and Social Services for Mentally Disordered Offenders and Others Requiring Similar Services: Final Summary Report.* London: HMSO.

DoH, HM Prison Service and National Assembly for Wales (2001) *Changing the Outlook: A Strategy for Developing and Modernising Mental Health Services in Prisons.* London: DoH.

Directorate of Health Care (1998) *Annual Report of the Directorate of Health Care 1996–1997.* London: The Stationery Office.

Directorate of Health Care (1999) *Annual Report of the Directorate of Health Care 1997–1998.* London: The Stationery Office.

Dooley, E. (1994) Unnatural death in prison: is there a future? In Liebling, A. and Ward, T. (Eds.) *Deaths in Custody: International Perspectives*. London: Whiting and Birch.

Drummer, R. (1996) Special needs: vulnerable prisoner care at Camphill, *Prison Service Journal*. 103: 44–6.

Edgar, K. and Rickford, D. (2003) Troubled inside: responding to the mental health needs of women prisoners. *Prison Report*. 62: 24–6.

Geary, R. (1980) *Deaths in Prison*, NCCL Briefing Paper, October. London: National Council for Civil Liberties.

Genders, E. and Player, E. (1995) *Grendon: A Study of a Therapeutic Prison*. Oxford: Clarendon Press.

Gostin, L. and Staunton, M. (1985) The case for prison standards: conditions of confinement, segregation, and medical treatment. In Vagg, J. Morgan, R. and Maguire, M. (Eds.) *Accountability and Prisons: Opening Up a Closed World*. London: Tavistock Publications.

Green, P. (1991) *Drug Couriers*. London: Howard League for Penal Reform.

Grounds, A. (1990) The mentally disordered in prison. *Prison Service Journal*. Winter: 29–40.

Grounds, A. (1994) Mentally disordered prisoners. In Player, E. and Jenkins, M. (Eds.) *Prisons After Woolf*. London: Routledge.

Grounds, A. (2000) The future of prison health care. *Journal of Forensic Psychiatry*. 11: 2, 260–7.

The Guardian, 30 September 2002, *Ministers Pledge Extra Funding for Prison Healthcare*.

The Guardian, 13 October 2002, *Lessons from a Prison Diary*.

Gunn, J., Maden, T. and Swinton, M. (1991) *Mentally Disordered Prisoners*. London: Home Office.

Hagel-Seymour, J. (1982) Environmental sanctuaries for susceptible prisoners. In Johnson, R. and Toch, H. (Eds.) *The Pains of Imprisonment*. Prospect Heights, IL: Waveland Press.

Harrison, C.A. and Abou Saleh, M.T. (2002) Psychiatric disorders and substance misuse: psychopathology. In Rassool, H. (Ed.) *Dual Diagnosis: Substance Misuse and Psychiatric Disorders*. Oxford: Blackwell Science.

Harvey, F. (2001) In pursuit of the healthy prison. *HLM*. 19: 1, 8–9.

Health Advisory Council for the Prison Service (1997) *The Provision of Mental Health Care in Prisons*. London: Prison Service.

HM Chief Inspector of Prisons (1990) *Report of a Review by Her Majesty's Chief Inspector of Prisons for England and Wales of Suicide and Self-Harm in Prison Service Establishments in England and Wales*. London: HMSO.

HM Chief Inspector of Prisons (1996) *Patient or Prisoner? A New Strategy for Health Care in Prisons*. London: Home Office.

HM Chief Inspector of Prisons (1999) *Suicide is Everyone's Concern: A Thematic Review by HM Chief Inspector of Prisons for England and Wales*. London: Home Office.

HM Chief Inspector of Prisons (2000a) *HM Prison Belmarsh: Report of a Short Unannounced Inspection, 6–7 December 1999*. London: Home Office.

HM Chief Inspector of Prisons (2000b) *Unjust Deserts: A Thematic Review of the Treatment and Conditions for Unsentenced Prisoners in England and Wales*. London: The Stationery Office.

HM Chief Inspector of Prisons (2001) *Report of a Full Announced Inspection of HMP Stafford, 16–20 July 2001*. London: The Stationery Office.

HM Chief Inspector of Prisons (2004) *Annual Report of HM Chief Inspector of Prisons for England and Wales 2002–2003*. London: The Stationery Office.

HM Prison Service (1997) *Caring for the Suicidal in Custody*. London: Prison Service.

HM Prison Service (2001a) *Prevention of Suicide and Self-Harm in the Prison Service*. London: Prison Service.

HM Prison Service (2001b) *Annual Report and Accounts: April 2000 to March 2001*. London: The Stationery Office.

HM Prison Service (2002a) *Prison Service Performance Standards*, available from *http://www.hmprisonservice.gov.uk/resourcecentre*

HM Prison Service (2002b) *Suicide and Self-Harm Prevention*, Prison Service Order 2700.

HM Prison Service (2003) *Annual Report and Accounts: April 2002 to March 2003*. London: The Stationery Office.

HM Prison Service website, 6 March 2002, *More Prisons to Offer Specialist Mental Health Services*, *http://www.hmprisonservice.gov.uk/news/news-text.asp?251*

Hodgins, S. and Côté, G. (1991) The mental health of penitentiary inmates in isolation. *Canadian Journal of Criminology*, April: 175–82.

Home Office (1997) *Imprisoned Women and Mothers*. London: Home Office.

Howard League (1999) *Desperate Measures: Prison Suicides and their Prevention*. London: The Howard League for Penal Reform.

Howard League (2004) Suicides in Prison 2003, *HLM*. 22: 1, 6.

Hussein Rassool, G. (2002) Substance use and dual diagnosis: concepts, theories and models. In Hussein Rassool, G. (Ed.) *Dual Diagnosis: Substance Misuse and Psychiatric Disorders*. Oxford: Blackwell Science.

Joint Committee on Human Rights (2004) *Deaths in Custody: Interim Report*. London: The Stationery Office.

Joint Prison Service and National Health Service Executive Working Group (Joint Working Group) (1999) *The Future Organisation of Prison Health Care*. London: DoH.

Keavney, P. (2001a) *Better Health Behind Bars is a Necessity*, 18 April 2001, *http://www.society.guardian.co.uk/crimeandpunishment/comment*

Keavney, P. (2001b) *Prison Medicine: A Crisis Waiting to Break*, BMA online, *http://web.bma.org.uk/public/pubother.nsf/webdoccsvw/prisons*, accessed 3 October 2001

Keavney, P. (2003) The crisis in prison healthcare. *Prison Report*. 62: 10–1.

King, R. and Morgan, R. (1980) *The Future of the Prison System*. Aldershot: Gower.

Levenson, J. (2000) *A Hard Act to Follow: Prisons and the Human Rights Act*. London: Prison Reform Trust.

Levenson, J. (2002) *Prison Overcrowding: The Inside Story*. London: Prison Reform Trust.

Liebling, A. (1992) *Suicides in Prison*. London: Routledge.

Liebling, A. (1999) Prison suicide and prisoner coping. In Tonry, M. and Petersilia, J. (Eds.) *Prisons, Crime and Justice: A Review of Research*, Vol. 26, Chicago: University of Chicago Press.

Liebling, A. and Krarup, H. (1993) *Suicide Attempts and Self-Injury in Male Prisons*. London: Home Office.

Lloyd, C. (1990) *Suicide and Self-Injury in Prison: A Literature Review*. Home Office Research Study 115, London: HMSO.

Marshall, T., Simpson, S. and Stevens, A. (2000) *Health Care in Prisons: A Health Care Needs Assessment*. Birmingham: University of Birmingham, Department of Public Health and Epidemiology.

McGauran, A. (2001) There's the Catch. *Health Service Journal*, February: 11–13.

Medlicott, D. (1999) *Researching the Prison: Prisoners as Knowledgeable Agents*. Unpublished paper presented to the British Criminology Conference 1999, Liverpool, 13–16 July.

Meltzer, H., Gill, B., Petticrew, M. and Hinds, K. (1995) *OPCS Surveys of Psychiatric Morbidity in Great Britain, Report 1: The Prevalence of Psychiatric Morbidity Among Adults Living in Private Households*. London: HMSO.

Miller, H.A. (1994) Re-examining psychological distress in the current conditions of segregation. *Journal of Correctional Health Care*. 1: 39–53.

Mills, A. (2002) Mental health in-reach: the way forward for prison? *Probation Journal*. 49: 2,: 107–19.

Mills, A. (2003) *Coping, Vulnerability and Disruption: Facilities for Prisoners with Special Needs*, unpublished PhD thesis, Cardiff University.

NACRO, Afro-Caribbean Mental Health Association and Commission for Racial Equality (1990) *Black People, Mental Health and the Courts*. London: NACRO.

NACRO (1993) *Women Leaving Prison*. London: NACRO.

Peay, J. (2002) Mentally disordered offenders, mental health, and crime. In Maguire, M., Morgan, R. and Reiner, R. (Eds.) *The Oxford Handbook of Criminology*, 3rd edn. Oxford: Oxford University Press.

Penal Affairs Consortium (1998) *An Unsuitable Place for Treatment: Diverting Mentally Disordered Offenders from Custody*. London: Penal Affairs Consortium.

Prison Health (2003) Transfer of Budget Responsibility, *Prison Heath, Q&As Issue*, 2nd March, available at *www.doh.gov.uk/prisonhealth*

Prison Reform Trust (2003a) First night in custody. *Prison Report*. 59: 18–9.

Reed, J. and Lyne, M. (1997) The quality of health care in prison: results of a year's programme of semi-structured inspections. *British Medical Journal*. 315: 1420–4.

Richer, A.D (1990) Should the prison medical service develop its role in the treatment of mentally ill offenders. *Prison Service Journal*. Winter: 15–8.

Safety Custody Group (2000) *Preventing Suicides and Making Prisons Safer For All Who Live and Work There*. London: Prison Service.

Safer Custody News (2002) Good Practice Guidance, 13: 1–3.

Sashidaran, S. (1989) Schizophrenic or just Black? *Community Care*. 5.10.89.

Seymour, J. (1992) Niches in prison. In Toch, H. *Living in Prison: The Ecology of Survival*. Washington DC: The American Psychological Association.

Sherratt, S. (1993) *Dying Inside: Suicides in Prison*. London: The Howard League for Penal Reform.

Shooter, M. (2001) *The National Mental Health Strategy*. Paper presented to NACRO conference on Mental Health and Crime: Punishment, Care and Civil Liberties, 22–23 March, University of Warwick.

Sim, J. (1990) *Medical Power in Prisons: The Prison Medical Service in England 1774–1989*. Milton Keynes: Open University Press.

Singleton, N., Meltzer, H. and Gatward, R. with Coid, J. and Deasy, D. (1998) *Psychiatric Morbidity Among Prisoners in England and Wales*. London: Office for National Statistics.

Social Exclusion Unit (2002) *Reducing Re-Offending by Ex-Prisoners*. London: Social Exclusion Unit.

Staite, C. (1995) Diversion from custody for mentally disordered offenders. *Prison Service Journal*. 95: 42–5.

Stevens, S. (1998) Inhumane containment. *Prison Report*. 4: 26–7.

Sykes, G.M. (1958) *The Society of Captives: A Study of a Maximum Security Prison*. Princeton, NJ: Princeton University Press.

Thurston, L., Lester, C. and Hamilton-Kirkwood, L. (2001) *HMP Cardiff Prison: Joint Health Needs Assessment 2001*. Bro Taff Health Authority Public Health and Policy.

Toch, H. (1992) *Living in Prison: The Ecology of Survival*. Washington DC: The American Psychological Association.

Toch, H. (1994) Prison violence in perspective. In Stanko, E. (Ed.) *Perspectives on Violence*. London: Quartet Books.

Toch, H. and Adams, K. (with Grant, J.D.) (1989) *Coping: Maladaptation in Prisons*. New Brunswick, NJ: Transaction Publishers.

Williams, H. (2002) Dual diagnosis – an overview: fact or fiction? In Hussein Rassool (Ed.) *Dual Diagnosis: Substance Misuse and Psychiatric Disorders*. Oxford: Blackwell Science.

Woolf, N. (1999) Shock results in the prison psychiatric census. *Prison Report*. 46: 6–7.

World Health Organisation (1998) *Mental Health Promotion in Prisons*. Report on a WHO Meeting, The Hague, Netherlands, 18–21 Nov. 1998.

Chapter 7

Mentally Vulnerable Adults in Prison: Specialist Resources and Practice

Alice Mills

Introduction

The previous chapter examined the types of problems encountered by prisoners with mental health problems. It also examined the history of policies dealing with mentally disordered prisoners, particularly in relation to the responsibilities of the Prison Service and NHS, and current provision to meet prisoners' needs. This chapter now focuses on the provision of specialist resources, regimes and practice to treat, care for and manage prisoners with mental health problems and those who are vulnerable to suicide or self-harm; it also looks at risk assessment procedures and issues surrounding the resettlement of prisoners into the community.

Special prison programmes

HMP Grendon

Several prisons offer specialist provisions to assist the management of mentally disordered prisoners and give them more specialised treatment. The therapeutic regime at HMP Grendon is perhaps the most famous example of this in the English and Welsh prison system. It operates as a therapeutic community and aims to facilitate and promote the welfare of each individual prisoner, by allowing them the opportunity to evaluate and understand their circumstances and behaviour, take responsibility for the consequences of their actions and develop alternative ways of acting (Genders and Player, 1995). Therapy takes the form of small group (six to eight prisoners) and community meetings, as well as individual sessions with psychiatrists, psychologists and doctors. Small group meetings address several common themes of self-esteem, sense of identity, personality, and relationships, particularly in relation to women, authority and each other. Meetings allow prisoners to learn from one another within a complex and varied system of relationships and interaction, and draw upon a wider range of life experiences and attitudes.

Prisoners with personality disorders are best suited to Grendon; those suffering from acute mental illness or who are 'highly disturbed' are not accepted, as all individuals must be able to accept responsibility for their own actions as part of the psychotherapeutic approach. Prisoners at Grendon also tend to be long-termers who have committed serious violent or sexual offences, as therapy takes about 19 months to complete, and prisoners must have at least 12 months of their sentence left to serve to be considered for a place here.

An evaluation of Grendon found that the majority of prisoners felt that they had benefited from the therapeutic regime as they had a greater understanding of themselves, their problems and others, and had gained self-confidence and felt less socially isolated. Grendon prisoners tend to have reduced rates of disciplinary offending, when they return to other establishments, although they may have difficulties readjusting to the mainstream prison system, which does not allow the same freedoms in terms of time out of cell, and where the 'traditional' prison culture prevails, which does not expect men to discuss their emotional problems (Genders and Player, 1995).

However, previous studies of re-offending amongst ex-Grendon prisoners have been rather mixed. Gunn et al. (1978) found that more than 80 per cent were reconvicted within ten years, but Cullen (1993) found that only 33 per cent were reconvicted within two years of release, a rate which dropped to 20 per cent amongst those who spent 18 months or longer in therapy. One of the approaches Grendon adopts has recently been accredited under 'What Works' criteria, suggesting that it has come within the crime reduction agenda (Peay, 2002), although it could be argued that reducing re-offending is not Grendon's primary aim. Grendon still seems to be the 'jewel' of the prison system, and there have been calls for its ethos and methods to be replicated elsewhere. This has now been achieved with the establishment of a new therapeutic community at a private prison, HMP Dovegate, which is currently undergoing evaluation, and a new therapeutic community within the women's section of HMP Winchester.

DSPD Unit at HMP Whitemoor

In 1999, the Green Paper *Managing Dangerous People with Severe Personality Disorder*, suggested that approximately 1,400 prisoners were at high risk of very serious offending, yet their needs were not met within the current system. Such prisoners are likely to be disruptive, and although some may benefit from therapeutic communities like HMP Grendon, they may not be effective for the most severely disordered (Bennett, 2003). As part of the recently formulated strategy on dangerous and severe personality disorders (DSPD), a unit was established at HMP Whitemoor in 2000 to offer a programme for this group of offenders to enable them to 'develop the skills and ability to better manage their personality and reduce their risk of re-offending' (Bennett, 2003). Suitable offenders for this unit are those who are likely to commit an offence that might lead to serious physical or psychological harm from which victims may find it difficult or impossible to recover. Like Grendon, the unit operates as a therapeutic environment with community meetings and group activities. It also provides work, education and clinical interventions based on a cognitive interpersonal model, delivered in group and one-to-one settings. Recent research has shown that the number of violent incidents occurring in the unit was much lower than expected, suggesting that these prisoners are being successfully managed here (Taylor, 2003). Yet considerable doubt has been raised by psychiatric practitioners about the treatability of such personality disorders and the category of 'dangerous and severe personality disorder' (DSPD) has been criticised for resting on moral ideas of 'dangerousness' rather than a clinical condition or diagnosis (Hudson, 2003).

Although not specifically designed for DSPD prisoners, a review of the use of the Close Supervision Centres (CSCs) at HMP Woodhill and HMP Durham by the Chief Inspector of Prisons speculated that they contained the extreme end of the 1,400 DSPD prisoners (HMCIP, 1999b). Thirty-three per cent on I wing at Durham and 59 per cent of those in the other units at Durham and Woodhill were diagnosed with psychopathic disorder. The centres are used to manage those prisoners who disrupt prison regimes by repeatedly challenging the authorities or committing acts of serious violence. However, the Chief Inspector suggested that they could be used to accommodate prisoners with DSPD, if they were based on a combination of control and treatment, with prisoners receiving mental health assessments to give a full picture of their needs, and an individual care and management plan is drawn up. One of these units, I wing at HMP Durham, already takes a similar approach, and aims to provide psychiatric and psychological assistance for those prisoners who are seen to be 'disturbed', but not sectionable under the Mental Health Act 1983. A psychiatric assessment is carried out on each prisoner, and a weekly plan of structured activity drawn up for them. Education, including basic skills, computing, food hygiene and art, takes place on the wing, and confident disciplined staff use their interpersonal skills to keep order and control. However, at the time of the review, this unit did not have in-house psychological support owing to recruitment difficulties, with the only psychiatric support coming from a part-time community psychiatric nurse (HMCIP, 1999b).

Services for prisoners at risk of suicide or self-harm: Listeners and First Night Centres

Recent years have seen the development of various initiatives to reduce the risk of suicide or self-harm among prisoners. The first Listener scheme was established in 1992 in HMP Swansea after the death of a 15-year-old prisoner. Listeners are prisoners who are specially selected and trained to befriend other prisoners and support those in distress, using sympathetic but active listening techniques (Davies, 1992; Sherratt, 1993; HM Prison Service, 1997; 2001; Liebling, 1999). It is recognised that prisoners may be better informed about how to cope with periods of despair, and there is an emphasis on helping prisoners to help themselves (HM Prison Service, 1997). Listeners are usually trained by the local Samaritans and supported by them through regular feedback sessions (Davies, 1992;, 1994; HM Prison Service, 2001). According to Davies (1992): 'For the prisoner who has difficulties relating to staff, their involvement can mean the difference between coping and simply giving up'. In the first year of the original Swansea scheme, the incidence of serious self-harm decreased by 50 per cent (Davies, 1992; 1994) and such schemes now exist in 81 per cent of prisons (HMCIP, 1999a), with the latest suicide prevention policy aiming to increase the number of Listeners in high risk prisons (HM Prison Service, 2001). However, it can be difficult for schemes to operate in local prisons and remand centres, where there is a high turnover of prisoners, and trained Listeners may be quickly transferred to other prisons (Prison Reform Trust, 1997). Furthermore, as all discussions with Listeners are completely confidential, this can lead to unease amongst staff who are not informed if prisoners tell Listeners that they intend to self-harm. On the other hand, prisoners may also distrust Listeners because they fear that they may discuss their problems with staff or other prisoners (HM Prison Service, 2001). Nevertheless, Listener schemes are seen to be a positive development by many prisoners and staff as they provide vital support and human contact (Howard League, 2003).

First Night in Custody schemes or centres have been set up in some prisons to care for prisoners in the first 24 hours of custody when they tend to be at greater risk of suicide. Their anxiety and sense of hopelessness may be particularly acute, and they may also be withdrawing from drugs or alcohol. The operation of these schemes varies from one prison to another, but they provide many types of practical and emotional assistance to support new prisoners and address their vulnerability. This may include assisting them with the process of adjusting to prison by offering advice and information, ensuring they understand the prison rules, and providing access to Listeners. A range of different prison services such as health care, probation, bail information, education, the chaplaincy, and community support agencies may also be involved; they may address concerns that the prisoner has about their family, relationships or housing, and allow them a phone call home (Safer Custody News, 2001). The First Night in Custody project at HMP Holloway works with the Bourne Trust, an organisation which helps prisoners and their families to face the problems caused by imprisonment. An evaluation of this scheme found that it was successful in reducing the immediate anxiety of women arriving in custody and resolving many of their immediate concerns, although sharing of information between prison staff and the scheme's workers was inconsistent and training could be improved (Prison Reform Trust, 2002). These schemes to support prisoners at what is often the most vulnerable and distressing time of their imprisonment are currently undergoing evaluation as part of the 'Safer Locals Programme' (see below), but it is uncertain when they will be rolled out across the prison estate.

Facilities for prisoners with special needs

Several prisons have established distinctive, segregative facilities for prisoners with special needs. There are many varying definitions of special needs, but prisoners accommodated here have a variety of problems which make it difficult for them to cope with prison life. Many have mental health problems, but they may also have severe drug or alcohol problems, learning difficulties, or even physical disabilities which make it difficult for them to move around prisons and participate in an active prison regime. Due to their special needs and their associated difficulties in coping with prison life, these prisoners tend to be vulnerable to suicide or self-harm, to victimisation by other prisoners, and violent outbursts because of their own frustrations. Such facilities act as 'halfway houses' between the main prison wings, where these prisoners may be victimised, or seen as 'disruptive' by prison staff due to their needs, and more specialist locations where they might be placed because of their vulnerabilities such as Rule 45 wings or VPUs, healthcare centres and segregation units, which can intensify the pains of imprisonment owing to the lack of opportunities to engage in constructive activity or associate with others (see above). These facilities, which generally accommodate between 40 and 50 prisoners, can protect prisoners from others who may wish to do them harm and offer them help from supportive staff, as well as more opportunities to participate in prison life.

Research into the effectiveness of these facilities at HMP Cardiff and HMP Camp Hill found that they helped prisoners to cope with prison life by providing 'niches' (Seymour, 1992); that is, ameliorative subsettings which are 'a potential instrument for the relaxation of stress and the achievement of psychological equilibrium' (Seymour, 1992). Prisoners found the atmosphere quieter there and more relaxed with fewer pressures than elsewhere in the prisons. Adjustment to prison life was made easier, as the unpredictability of the prisoner world and the risk of violence was reduced by their more sheltered setting, and prisoners reported feeling much safer here than they did in other parts of the prisons (Mills, 2003).

Staff working in these facilities made a substantial contribution to creating these 'niches'. Small teams of officers worked there regularly to maintain continuity of staffing, and although they received little or no extra training, they were specially selected for their more sympathetic approach. Having regular staff working on the facilities meant that better staff-prisoner relations could be built up and officers were well placed to notice any changes or differences in a prisoner's mental or physical state. They also recognised the need to try to understand prisoners' complex problems and be tolerant of their behaviour rather than resorting to inappropriate disciplinary responses, which might worsen their coping difficulties. Many encouraged prisoners to talk to them about their concerns in the hope of alleviating their distress. Such talk has been described as an 'invaluable aspect of care' (Medlicott, 2001; see also Dooley, 1994) and prisoners clearly appreciated the regular officers' approachable, friendly manner. Between 25 and 40 per cent reported that they would talk to these officers about personal problems (Mills, 2003), and although these figures do not appear to be high, another study of prisoners at risk of suicide found that only a fifth would discuss a problem with anyone (including staff, prisoners and others) (Liebling, 1992).

Prisoners in the facility at Camp Hill received more specialist assistance with their individual special needs, including special education classes to improve their basic and life skills, and access to a community psychiatric nurse. Participation in constructive activity such as work or education can benefit those with a wide range of mental health problems and can improve self-esteem as well as preparing prisoners for their release, and the education classes had received praise from outside consultants for empowering those with chronic mental health problems to obtain some qualifications. Classrooms and workshops may provide a temporary respite from the pressures of imprisonment and the classes were highly rated by over three-quarters of the prisoners, not only because they were able to improve their basic skills, but also because of the understanding and tolerant approach of the teachers working there, with whom they felt able to discuss their problems without fear of being judged.

Nevertheless, these facilities could do much more to help prisoners with special needs, and the new multi-disciplinary mental health in-reach teams could certainly play a part here, particularly as many of these prisoners have multiple needs. Daycare could be provided on the facilities and could include programmes to teach these prisoners coping skills, as well as life skills and ways to improve their self-esteem. These could be developed and delivered by prison officers, and education and psychology staff as well as psychiatric staff, particularly as many of the prisoners accommodated on the facilities were unsuitable for offending behaviour programmes such as Enhanced Thinking Skills (ETS) due to their mental health problems and poor basic skills (see below). Drug treatment workers from the local CARATS (Counselling, Assessment, Referral, Advice and Treatment Services) who at the time of the research did not play a specific role within either of the two facilities, could also participate in this approach to ensure that the needs of prisoners who misuse substances or have dual diagnosis are met (Mills, 2003).

Despite the potential of such good practice initiatives, for managing and caring for prisoners with mental health problems, because they have been established by individual prisons, rather than on a nationwide basis, they are likely to be vulnerable to funding shortages, population pressures, staff changes, and governors' changing priorities.

Risk assessment and management procedures

Transfer to NHS facilities

As noted above, it is government policy that 'wherever possible, mentally disordered persons should receive care and treatment from the health and social services' (Home Office, 1990, Circular 60/90) rather than from custodial settings, a view shared by many others who agree that mentally disordered offenders should be cared for within the NHS or other institutions such as specialist hostels (Wilson, 1980; Ross and Bingley, 1985; Gunn et al., 1991; Woolf, 1991; DoH/Home Office, 1992; Stern, 1993; Phipps, 1994; NACRO, 1995; Penal Affairs Consortium, 1998). Sections 47 and 48 of the Mental Health Act 1983 allow for sentenced and remand prisoners respectively to be transferred to a psychiatric hospital, special hospital or regional secure unit. Under section 47, the prisoner must be suffering from mental illness, severe mental impairment, mental impairment or psychopathic disorder. It must be appropriate for them to be detained in hospital and two doctors (one of whom must be a psychiatrist) must certify that such conditions have been met. For remand prisoners, under section 48, there must be mental illness or severe mental impairment and the prisoner must be in urgent need of treatment. Transfer to NHS facilities may be difficult because of a lack of suitable medium-secure beds. Despite recommendations from the Glancy report in 1974 which suggested that 1,000 beds should be available, and the Butler report in 1975 which recommended the provision of 2,000 beds, the Reed report found that only 600 had been made available by 1992, and recommended that 1,500 beds should be made available nationally, with new regional targets set according to need. Increased longer-term medium-secure provision was also proposed as Regional Secure Units only hold patients for up to 18–24 months and many mentally disordered offenders are therefore held inappropriately in special hospitals, as they are the only long term provision available (DoH/Home Office, 1992).

In recent years, it has become easier to transfer prisoners to the NHS (Reed and Lyne, 1997; HMCIP, 2004). By 1995, 1,250 places in medium-secure units were available, and the number of transfers almost quadrupled between 1984 and 1994, largely owing to a twelvefold increase in the number of transfers of remand prisoners (Health Advisory Council for the Prison Service (HAC), 1997). However, the number of transfers remained constant between 1993 and 1997 (Directorate of Health Care, 1999), and Reed's target of 1,500 medium secure beds was formulated at a time when the prison population stood at just under 45,000, so the need is now likely to be greater due to the rise in the prison population. In 2001, 2,383 NHS secure places were available, yet Peay (2002) suggests that there were approximately 4,648 prisoners who had functional psychosis at this time, and were in need of treatment and possibly in need of transfer to hospital. There are currently up to 500 patients in prison health care centres who are sufficiently ill to require admission to the NHS (Joint Committee on Human Rights, 2004), and although the number of secure beds is due to be increased further (HM Prison Service, 2000), it seems unlikely to meet the demand for them, particularly if the number of mentally disordered prisoners keeps rising.

Prisoners who have been accepted for transfer to the NHS should now be transferred within three months of assessment (HMCIP, 2004), although in the community they would be admitted within 24 hours (Gunn et al., 1991; PAC, 1998). Delays can occur for several reasons such as waiting for a consultant psychiatrist to conduct an assessment, disputes over the correct level of security, difficulties in identifying a patient's catchment area and therefore funding for their assessment and care, and a shortage of beds in some areas of the country (Gunn et al., 1991; HAC, 1997; Bean, 2001). Psychiatric staff may have difficulties visiting prisoners because of the distance they may have to travel, or being kept waiting for long periods of time at the prison and they may have to cancel clinics in order to be able to see prisoners at a time that is convenient to the prison regime (HAC, 1997; PAC, 1998; Bean, 2001). Transfer is a complex process requiring communication between prison staff, outside psychiatric staff and the Home Office, and it has been suggested that prison staff may have little incentive to push for transfer unless the prisoner is demonstrably mentally disordered and exhibits florid symptoms or excessively disruptive behaviour (Kennedy and Truman, 2000).

One of the biggest obstacles to transferring prisoners remains the refusal of NHS staff to accept them as patients if they are seen as potentially violent or disruptive, and there may be a perception that at least in prison, they are subject to a secure environment (DoH et al., 2001). They may be sent back to prison if they are disruptive, yet be viewed as disturbed by prison authorities and thus sent to hospital, resulting in them being 'bussed' between health care services and prison (Toch, 1983; see also Wilson, 1980). Other offenders may not be thought susceptible to treatment and approximately one in ten transferred prisoners are returned because clinical staff have concluded that they suffer from a personality disorder or substance misuse problem rather than mental illness (Kennedy and Truman, 2000). Clearly then, there are many people in prison who should not be there due to their mental health problems, and whom prisons are not equipped to deal with, yet neither the NHS nor the prison system is prepared to take responsibility for them, with each service viewing it as a problem to be addressed by the other; thus prisoners are left to fall through the gaps in provision.

Suicide prevention policies

Suicide in prison has become a major concern in recent years owing to the increase in the number of suicides and incidents of self-harm, despite a variety of policies to improve the assessment and care of prisoners at risk of such acts. When a prisoner is felt to be at risk, an F2052SH form should be opened on them (HM Prison Service, 1997) and the prisoner should then see the doctor within 24 hours, and a case conference involving a multi-disciplinary team should be held to draw up a support plan. The case should be regularly reviewed, and the F2052SH should note any supervision or support given and travel with the prisoner whenever escorted or transferred outside the prison. It should only be closed when the prisoner is no longer perceived to be at risk. This system has been widely criticised, as four-fifths of those who commit suicide in prison are not on an open form (HM Prison Service, 2001). This may be because it was not recognised that these prisoners were in distress, or staff may have been deterred from opening a form by the paperwork involved; however, it may indicate that the system is successful in caring for those who are vulnerable (Howard League, 1999).

Reviews of the 1994 suicide awareness policy, which introduced the F2052SH system, found that whilst it encouraged a multi-disciplinary approach and created widespread awareness of suicide and self-harm issues amongst staff, it had not been properly implemented, many staff had not received training and appropriate measures such as case conferences and individual care plans were not being taken (HMCIP, 1999a; HM Prison Service, 2001; see also HMCIP, 2004). Some prisons had developed good supportive local policies, but in others there was little to offer prisoners in the way of constructive activity and specialist resources or services such as counselling or therapeutic provision. Furthermore, the focus on awareness could lead to over-inclusiveness with many prisoners being on F2052SHs and staff being unable to concentrate their time and attention on those at greater risk. An evaluation of the operation of F2052SHs by Manchester University and the Institute of Psychiatry (published on Prison Service Quantum website) has, however, suggested that approximately 20 per cent of prisoners in female and local prisons are sufficiently at risk of suicide to warrant being on an F2052SH, representing an increase of between three and seven times the number that are actually opened, and so demonstrating that the F2052SH system is actually under-used. The evaluation also found that although formal pro-cedures were followed correctly, the more qualitative aspects of the system were somewhat lacking. Prisoners often did not know that they had a care or support plan, and no one member of staff had responsibility for ensuring that elements of the care plan were actually implemented. Information was often written in either F2052SHs or Prisoner Medical Records (PMRs) rather than in both, leaving gaps in information and showing a lack of cohesion in the multi-disciplinary approach. Staff were also found to be reluctant to close F2052SHs. This may have affected the opportunities that at-risk prisoners were able to access, particularly as some prisons are reluctant to accept those prisoners on an open F2052SH. Additionally, many prisoners disliked being on such a form as they were deprived of any privacy by having to share a cell, and felt stigmatised by other prisoners.

The most recent Prison Service suicide prevention policy was introduced in 2001 and represents a shift from the broader focus on suicide awareness (HM Prison Service, 1997) to one on prevention and risk assessment. It recom-mends that whilst all prisoners should be supported, more resources should be invested in prisons with high risk prisoners, and it launched the Safer Locals Programme to pilot new suicide prevention measures at five local prisons which have had a high number of suicides. (HMP Eastwood Park, HMPYOI Feltham, HMP Leeds, HMP Wandsworth, HMP Winchester). This programme aims to improve the identification of risk, reduce prisoner anxiety, provide a safer physical environment and supportive relationships. Measures include new guidelines on the support, treatment and observation of at-risk prisoners, increased numbers of prisoner Listeners, and enhanced staff training in high risk locations including mental health training for staff in local prisons and those working on specialist locations such as VPUs. The assessment regime on induction should also be full, and prisoners should be given an opportunity to contact their families on reception. As substance misusers are at a high risk of suicide, particularly when they are withdrawing from the substance they have been misusing, detoxification units are recommended to provide a suitable, supportive environment in which to do this (HM Prison Service, 2001). Additionally, one staff member should be responsible for assessing the prisoner, and preparing and implementing a care plan, with support from the new mental heath in-reach staff (PSO 2700, HM Prison Service, 2002). Initial results from an evaluation of the Safer Locals Programme suggest that mental health in-reach teams, day care, first night centres, relevant training and improved environments have a positive impact on prisoner distress (Liebling et al., 2003). However, this strategy does not appear to have reduced the number of suicides which rose by 40 per cent between 2001–2 and 2002–03 (Solomon, 2003).

In light of the review of the F2052SH system, a new assessment system is currently being piloted in five prisons (HMP and YOI Low Newton, HMPYOI Feltham, HMP Wandsworth, HMP Holme House, HMP and YOI Woodhill), to be implemented nationally in late 2004. Assessment Care in Custody and Teamwork (ACCT) aims to promote better joined-up approaches to care and to improve multi-disciplinary working to provide more support for residential staff and make better use of the new specialist mental health resources. It acknowledges that 'the key to reducing risk is helping prisoners to solve their problems and making them feel supported and cared for' (HMP Wandsworth internal document, published on Prison Service Quantum website); it also recognises the need to bolster their self-esteem, address any immediate problems and improve their sense of hope for the future. Prisoners are to be engaged in discussions about what might help them, and there is also increased stress on the assessment of problems and needs to ensure that prisoners with different needs, such as those who self-harm without suicidal intent, receive different care. ACCT requires members of staff to complete a *concern and keep safe form* on a prisoner whom they feel is at risk of suicide r self-harm. Within 24 hours, members of the specially trained ACCT response team will interview the distressed prisoner and the unit manager will chair a case review, where it will be decided whether the prisoner is at high, medium or low risk of suicide (Safer Custody Group, Prison Service Quantum website). If at low risk, prisoners will be supported in the same way that they were on F2052SHs, but if at medium or high risk, they will receive a full psychosocial assessment to inform staff as to what will support the prisoner and keep them safe. A care plan based on this will then be drawn up with an agreed review date.

Staff training

As they are likely to have the most contact with mentally disordered and vulnerable prisoners, it has been suggested that prison officers should be given training in recognising and dealing with mental illness in order to contribute to better care of these prisoners (WHO, 1998). Training in mental heath problems is now provided to new prison officer recruits and, as part of the Safer Locals Programme, to front line staff in local prisons (HM Prison

Service, 2001). However, training in the new ACCT system will be focused primarily on case managers and assessors, with basic grade staff receiving only a briefing on the new system (Safer Custody Group, Prison Service website). If mental health and particularly vulnerability towards suicide are, in the words of the former Chief Inspector of Prisons 'everyone's concern' (HMCIP, 1999a), then such training on these issues should be perhaps rolled out to all prison officers, as well as other members of staff such as chaplains, teachers and members of the Independent Monitoring Boards (previously known as Boards of Visitors), so that they are all able to recognise vulnerability and provide help to those at risk.

Pre-release programmes and resettlement issues

Prisoners with mental health problems are often caught in the so-called *revolving door* of offending, institutionalisation, and lack of community support (Wilson, 1980; Barker and Swyer, 1995; NACRO, 1995). They may be persistent recidivists, and despite many calls to stop the revolving door from spinning, they are often excluded from various provisions which might help to stop their re-offending. Firstly, many of these prisoners are unable to participate in accredited offending behaviour programmes, such as Enhanced Thinking Skills, which aim to change the way offenders think and act and give them skills to avoid offending behaviour. They are targeted at particular groups of offenders, such as sex offenders, high risk violent offenders, and offenders who need to develop their anger management skills or their reasoning and problem-solving skills. The Prison Service aims to ensure that 7,100 prisoners complete these courses every year (HM Prison Service, 2003), but certain groups of prisoners including short-term prisoners, those with poor basic skills, or those with mental health problems, are excluded from such programmes, often because it is thought that they would not be able to cope with their style and intensity (SEU, 2002). Clearly if approximately 90 per cent of the prison population has some sort of mental disorder, then a significant amount of prisoners are unable to take advantage of this kind of opportunity to reduce their chances of re-offending. Even if they do manage to access such programmes, their chances of successfully completing the programme may be reduced if they do not receive support for their mental health problem.

Secondly, mentally disordered prisoners may face additional difficulties when released. They may find it even more difficult to access housing and employment; although accommodation schemes may provide support for those with mental health needs, they may be excluded from social housing because their support needs are seen to be too great (DETR, 2001), and have their job applications rejected due to their mental health history. Ex-prisoners can be considered a priority for local authority housing if they have written evidence from a psychiatrist that they have mental health problems. However, this measure is not widely used and a survey by the HM Inspectorates of Prisons and Probation (2001) found that only seven per cent of prisoners interviewed had been given such a letter when previously released from prison. Several voluntary groups such as NACRO and the Revolving Doors Agency do help ex-prisoners to find accommodation with varying levels of support. For example, the Southside Project takes prisoners from a number of London prisons to appointments with the Benefits Agency and helps them to find suitable housing. Unfortunately, such work tends to be based on small, local initiatives rather than being available on a nationwide basis, and often only has short-term funding. There is therefore a need for more statutory arrangements for this vulnerable group, particularly as Swyer and Lart (1996) have suggested that 'housing is the passport to many resources in the community'. Homeless ex-prisoners can have difficulties accessing suitable care and treatment on release, as they may not be able to register with a GP, and community mental healthcare services in their home area may not be willing to supply services to them on the basis that they are not resident there (Swyer and Lart., 1996; Mills, 2002).

As well as housing problems, other factors can affect the organisation of mental health care for prisoners on release into the community. Information sharing and assistance between prisons and community agencies such as GPs and care co-ordinators have been somewhat lacking, particularly for short term prisoners, as there may not be time to organise such co-ordination of care before they are released, and any consultation between agencies may be hampered by patient confidentiality (HAC, 1997).

Several measures can improve these resettlement arrangements and offer better continuity of care on release. The Care Programme Approach (CPA) provides a framework for caring for people with severe mental illness and ensures that they receive systematic assessment, and planned and co-ordinated community health and social care (HAC, 1997; Swyer and Lart, 1996). It should help to smooth the transition from the community to custody and back, as those who are on a care plan before entering prison should be able to continue their programmes of treatment, with care co-ordinators retaining contact with them during their imprisonment. The new mental health in-reach teams should liaise with mental health staff responsible for prisoners' care in the community to help prisoners to engage with the appropriate services when they are released (DoH et al., 2001). However, ensuring that offenders receive such care may be problematic. As the funding allocated to mental health in-reach teams will go to the PCTs which have prisons in their area (DoH et al., 2001), those areas without prisons within their boundaries will not receive any extra money, making it less likely that they will be willing to co-ordinate and offer services for ex-prisoners with mental health problems (Mills, 2002). Furthermore, community mental health professionals working in a prison in one region may not have any influence, connections or access to facilities in another, which may create difficulties in organising provision for prisoners who are accommodated a long way from their home area. Probation officers in the community and in prison could, however, bring together healthcare staff from the prison and the prisoner's home area and use their knowledge of the available services in order to facilitate the transition between mental healthcare services. One example of this was an initiative at HMP Brixton, where a specialist probation officer was employed part-time as part of the multi-agency in-reach services. The officer had a mental health background, was funded by the local health authority, and liaised with outside probation officers in all areas of the country regarding the resettlement needs of individual prisoners including housing and mental healthcare. Enquiries were made as to whether or not the prisoner was already known to mental health services in their local area and if not, how such services could be accessed. Sadly, this initiative has now closed down as the probation officer left to move to another position, and this exemplifies the transitory and vulnerable nature of good practice initiatives, as discussed earlier. Any services involving probation services are likely to exclude short-sentence prisoners, although proposals in the Halliday report on sentencing to extend supervision in the community (Home Office, 2001) may ensure that these prisoners do receive assistance. Until extensive resettlement assistance is available for all prisoners, and until PCTs in different parts of the country are prepared to make provision for those who may not have lived in their region for some time, it seems likely that prisoners with mental health problems will continue to be caught in the 'revolving door' of offending and imprisonment.

Summary of main points

This chapter has examined some of the specialist initiatives that have been established to help prisoners with a range of different mental health problems and to reduce vulnerability to suicide or self-harm. With the exception of the Listeners, many of these services are limited to certain groups of prisoners and only exist in certain prisons rather than being available throughout the system. Prisoners who may benefit from them may therefore be unable to access them, and the services themselves can be vulnerable to funding shortages and changing priorities, which may affect their operation or even lead to their closure.

Risk assessment and management procedures have improved in recent years, although there is still a need for caution when evaluating their effectiveness. Transferring prisoners to the NHS appears to have become easier, yet the transfer process is still hampered by factors such as the shortage of medium-secure beds, delays in clarifying financial responsibilities, and the refusal of NHS staff to accept prisoners who they deem to be potentially violent or disruptive. This may leave some prisoners who clearly fall within the confines of the Mental Health Act 1983, to be accommodated in prisons that are not equipped to care for them, and it seems that they belong in neither the mental health nor the criminal justice system. Developments in suicide prevention policies should mean that at-risk prisoners are better identified and supported; and the Safer Locals Programme has been shown to reduce prisoner distress. However, the number of suicides is still rising, and the value of such policies may be limited if only certain members of staff receive training in such matters.

Prisoners with mental health problems are often excluded from provisions to help to reduce their chances of re-offending. Many offending behaviour programmes are unsuitable for them and they may suffer considerable problems trying to resettle in the community and accessing services there, often due to their lack of accommodation. Although the CPA should help to ensure that prisoners receive mental health treatment on their release, like so many other initiatives, such an approach only deals with those with a serious mental illness, thus excluding a large number of prisoners with more common, less serious mental disorders.

Conclusions: implications for policy and practice

Clearly then there has been considerable debate and discussion regarding the care of mentally disordered prisoners, with many commentators agreeing that they should not be in prison at all, particularly as imprisonment can cause or exacerbate mental disorder. Indeed, Kennedy and Truman (2000) have gone as far as suggesting that detaining a person in a non-therapeutic prison environment whilst they are mentally ill could be seen to be degrading treatment under Article 3 of the Human Rights Act. However, it is uncertain as to whether this should lead to mentally disordered prisoners not being imprisoned or to an improvement in mental health provision to ensure that prison is not a 'non-therapeutic' environment. Ironically, if the Prison Service did improve its services for this group, there is a danger that sentencers might be encouraged to send such people to prison rather than diverting them to the NHS, or prisons might be turned into 'dumping grounds' of patients that the NHS are unwilling to accept (NACRO, 1995; Prins, 1995; Staite, 1995).

Yet improved mental health care services undoubtedly need to be provided both in prison and in the community if prisoners' mental health needs are to be sufficiently met and the revolving door is to stop turning. The specialist prison programmes and services discussed in this chapter and the establishment of mental health in-reach teams could be seen as a positive step in this direction. However, the in-reach teams may suffer from staff recruitment problems and may develop on a rather ad hoc basis due to a lack of any kind of evidence base to support different service models (Birmingham and Kendall, personal communication). Furthermore, they tend to provide treatment for only a small proportion of prisoners with severe mental disorders, meaning that prisoners with less serious mental health problems will not receive any specialist care. In order to treat all prisoners with humanity, improve their general well-being, and reduce their vulnerability, there is a need for all prison establishments to be 'healthy prisons' (HMCIP, 1999a). This would help to alleviate the pains of imprisonment, such as boredom, isolation and fear of others, which can exacerbate mental health problems and vulnerability to suicide and self-harm, as well as providing a supportive environment to promote the mental health of the prisoners, and staff, who live and work within the prison system.

References

Barker, M. and Swyer, B. (1995) The experience of the Wessex project. *Prison Service Journal*. 95: 45–8.

Bean, P. (2001) *Mental Disorder and Community Safety*. Basingstoke: Palgrave.

Bennett, J. (2003) DSPD Units at HMP Whitemoor. *Criminal Justice Matters*. 51, Spring: 22–3.

Cullen, E. (1993) The Grendon Reconviction Study Part I. *Prison Service Journal*. 90: 35–7.

Davies, B. (1992) Suicide awareness: the Listener Scheme at Swansea. In *Perspectives on Prison: A Collection of Views on Prison Life and Running Prisons*. London: HMSO.

Davies, B. (1994) The Swansea Listener Scheme: views from the prison landings. *The Howard League*. 33: 2, 125–36.

DETR (2001) *Housing: Local Authority Policy and Practice on Allocations, Transfers and Homelessness*. London: DETR.

DoH/Home Office (1992) *Review of Health and Social Services for Mentally Disordered Offenders and Others Requiring Similar Services: Final Summary Report*. London: HMSO.

DoH, HM Prison Service and National Assembly for Wales (2001) *Changing the Outlook: A Strategy for Developing and Modernising Mental Health Services in Prisons*. London: DoH.

Directorate of Health Care (1999) *Annual Report of the Directorate of Health Care 1997–1998*. London: The Stationery Office.

Dooley, E. (1994) Unnatural death in prison: is there a future? In Liebling, A. and Ward, T. (Eds.) *Deaths in Custody: International Perspectives*. London: Whiting and Birch.

Genders, E. and Player, E. (1995) *Grendon: A Study of a Therapeutic Prison*. Oxford: Clarendon Press.

Gunn, J., Maden, T. and Swinton, M. (1991) *Mentally Disordered Prisoners*. London: Home Office.

Gunn, J., Robertson, G., Dell, S. and Way, C. (1978) *Psychiatric Aspects of Imprisonment*. London: Academic Press.

Health Advisory Council for the Prison Service (1997) *The Provision of Mental Health Care in Prisons*. London: Prison Service.

HM Chief Inspector of Prisons (1999a) *Suicide is Everyone's Concern: A Thematic Review by HM Chief Inspector of Prisons for England and Wales*. London: Home Office.

HM Chief Inspector of Prisons (1999b) *Inspection of Close Supervision Centres, August–September 1999: A Thematic Inspection by Her Majesty's Chief Inspector of Prisons*. London: Home Office.

HM Chief Inspector of Prisons (2001) *Report of a Full Announced Inspection of HMP Stafford, 16–20 July 2001*. London: Home Office.

HM Chief Inspector of Prisons (2004) *Annual Report of HM Chief Inspector of Prisons for England and Wales 2002–2003*. London: The Stationery Office.

HM Inspectorates of Prisons and Probation (2001) *Through the Prison Gate: A Joint Thematic Review by HM Inspectorates of Prisons and Probation*. London: Home Office.

HM Prison Service (1997) *Caring for the Suicidal in Custody*. London: Prison Service.

HM Prison Service (2000) *Annual Report and Accounts: April 1999 to March 2000*. London: The Stationery Office.

HM Prison Service (2001) *Prevention of Suicide and Self-Harm in the Prison Service*. London: Prison Service.

HM Prison Service (2002) *Suicide and Self-harm Prevention*. PSO 2700. London: Prison Service.

HM Prison Service (2003) *Annual Report and Accounts: April 2002 to March 2003*. London: The Stationery Office.

HM Prison Service website, 6 March 2002, *More Prisons to Offer Specialist Mental Health Services, http://www.hmprisonservice.gov.uk/news/newstext.asp?251*

Home Office (1990) *Provision for Mentally Disordered Offenders*. Home Office Circular No. 66/90.

Home Office (2001) *Making Punishments Work: Report of a Review of the Sentencing Framework for England and Wales*. London: Home Office.

Howard League (1999) *Desperate Measures: Prison Suicides and their Prevention*. London: The Howard League for Penal Reform.

Howard League (2003) *Suicide and Self-Harm Prevention: The Management of Self-Injury in Prisons*. London: Howard League for Penal Reform.

Hudson, B. (2003) Detaining dangerous offenders: dangerous confusions and dangerous politics. *Criminal Justice Matters*. 51, Spring: 14–5.

Joint Committee on Human Rights (2004) *Deaths in Custody: Interim Report*. London: The Stationery Office.

Kennedy, M. and Truman, C. (2000) Prisoners with mental disorders. In Leech, M. and Cheney, D. (Eds.) *The Prisons Handbook 2000*. Winchester: Waterside Press.

Liebling, A. (1992) *Suicides in Prison*. London: Routledge.

Liebling, A. (1999) Prison suicide and prisoner coping. In Tonry, M. and Petersilia, J. (Eds.) *Prisons, Crime and Justice: A Review of Research*. Chicago: University of Chicago Press.

Liebling, A., Durie, L., van der Beukel, A., Harvey, J. and Tait, S. (2003) How safe is safe. *Prison Report*. 62: 13–4.

Medlicott, D. (1999) *Researching the Prison: Prisoners as Knowledgeable Agents*. Unpublished paper presented to the British Criminology Conference 1999, Liverpool, 13–16 July.

Medlicott, D. (2001) *Surviving the Prison Place: Narratives of Suicidal Prisoners*. Aldershot: Ashgate.

Meltzer, H., Gill, B., Petticrew, M. and Hinds, K. (1995) *OPCS Surveys of Psychiatric Morbidity in Great Britain, Report 1: The Prevalence of Psychiatric Morbidity Among Adults Living in Private Households*. London: HMSO.

Mills, A. (2002) Mental health in-reach: the way forward for prison? *Probation Journal*. 49: 2, 107–19.

Mills, A. (2003) *Coping, Vulnerability and Disruption: Facilities for Prisoners with Special Needs*, unpublished PhD thesis, Cardiff University.

NACRO (1995) *Mentally Disturbed Prisoners*. London: NACRO.

Peay, J. (2002) Mentally disordered offenders, mental health, and crime. In Maguire, M., Morgan, R. and Reiner, R. (Eds.) *The Oxford Handbook of Criminology*, 3rd edn. Oxford: Oxford University Press.

Phipps, A.J. (1994) Mentally disordered offenders. *Prison Service Journal*. 95: 50–2.

Prins, H. (1995) *Offenders, Deviants or Patients?* London: Routledge.

Prison Reform Trust (1997) *The Rising Toll of Prison Suicide*. London: Prison Reform Trust.

Prison Reform Trust (2002) First night in custody. *Prison Report*. 59: 18–9.

Reed, J. and Lyne, M. (1997) The quality of health care in prison: results of a year's programme of semi-structured inspections. *British Medical Journal*. 315: 1420–4.

Ross, J. and Bingley, W. (1985) Mentally abnormal offenders and prison medicine. In Prison Reform Trust (1985) *Prison Medicine: Ideas on Health Care in Penal Establishments*. London: Prison Reform Trust.

Safer Custody News (2001) *First Night in Custody*. 3: 2–5

Seymour, J. (1992) Niches in prison. In Toch, H. *Living in Prison: The Ecology of Survival*. Washington DC: The American Psychological Association.

Sherratt, S. (1993) *Dying Inside: Suicides in Prison*. London: The Howard League for Penal Reform.

Social Exclusion Unit (2002) *Reducing Re-Offending by Ex-Prisoners*. London: SEU.

Solomon, E. (2003) *A Measure of Success: An Analysis of the Prison Service's Performance against its Key Performance Indicators 2002–03*. London: Prison Reform Trust.

Staite, C. (1995) Diversion from custody for mentally disordered offenders. *Prison Service Journal*. 95: 42–5.

Stern, V. (1993) *Bricks of Shame: Britain's Prisons*. London: Penguin.

Swyer, B. and Lart, R. (1996) Prisoners' mental health problems: screening needs and accessing services. *Probation Journal*. 43: 4, 205–10.

Taylor, R. (2003) *An Assessment of Violent Incident Rates in the Dangerous Severe Personality Unit at HMP Whitemoor, Home Office Research Findings No. 210*. London: Home Office.

Toch, H. (1983) The disturbed disruptive inmate: where does the bus stop? *The Journal of Psychiatry and Law*. Fall 1982: 327–49.

Wilson, R. (1980) Who will care for the 'mad and bad'. *Corrections Magazine*. 6: 5–17.

Woolf, Lord Justice (1991) *Prison Disturbances April 1990: Report of an Inquiry by the Rt. Hon. Lord Justice Woolf (Parts I and II) and His Honour Stephen Tumin (Part II)*. London: HMSO.

Chapter 8

Diversion from Custody

Phil Woods

Introduction

The diversion of mentally disordered people from the criminal justice system to mental health services, either prior to or following sentencing, is not a new concept. Its history can certainly be traced back to the 1800s. More recently the drive for diverting the mentally disordered gained momentum following a government circular (Home Office, 1990) and a review of services for mentally disordered offenders by Dr Reed (DoH and Home Office, 1993) advocated that wherever possible a mentally disordered offender (or alleged offender) should receive care and treatment from services other than those provided by the criminal justice system. This policy continues, as a result of which numerous court liaison schemes have evolved with the aim of identifying the mentally disordered offender in need of mental health care rather than custodial care either prior to the court, from the court, or from remand and prison. This Reed review (DoH and Home Office, 1993) called for continuity of care with multi-disciplinary care teams consisting of general practitioners, forensic and general psychiatrists, nurses, approved and generic social workers, probation officers, clinical psychologists, occupational therapists, speech therapists, other therapists, interpretators, and education staff. Specific recommendations also included that there should be a nation-wide provision of properly resourced court assessment schemes; where a psychiatrist, community psychiatric nurse or approved social worker assess suspected mentally disordered offenders and advise the court on non-custodial alternatives (Phipps, 1994). Further recommendations were for the forensic training of community psychiatric nurses.

The practice of diversion from custody

McKittrick and Eysenck (1984) define diversion from custody as 'the halting or suspending of proceedings against an accused person in favour of processing through a non-criminal disposal'. It is well acknowledged that diversion can occur in a number of ways, either following arrest, from

Magistrates' court, following remand into custody, at sentencing, or following a custodial sentence.

In practice the process should involve the identification of mentally disordered offenders at the point of arrest and if possible diverting the individual from a custodial remand to a place where further assessment and treatment can be obtained. Therefore, when appearing at court for sentencing, with all the information available on that individual the court is able to make an order concerning treatment which is more formal and binding.

The point at which diversion occurs depends largely on whether the Crown Prosecution Service is prepared to discontinue criminal proceedings. Its decision must take account of several factors, including: the severity of the offence, circumstances surrounding the offence, the likely penalty, the age of the offender (too young, old, or infirm), the complainant's attitude, and presence of mental illness or stress (Prins, 1992). According to Hillis (1999):

> . . . *all those whose mental health problems culminate in their becoming entangled in the criminal justice system should, as a matter of principle, be diverted into the appropriate healthcare services. Where this is not possible, there should be provision for appropriate mental healthcare within police custody and during the transition between court and provision, whether they be remanded and convicted.*

In the case of the more serious, violent, mentally disordered offender, it is almost inevitable that they will spend a period in custody either awaiting a psychiatric report, or transfer for further assessment or treatment (Joseph, 1990; Robertson. et al., 1994). Furthermore, due to legislation within the Bail Act 1976 the mentally disordered offender is more likely than the non-mentally disordered offender to be remanded into custody, indeed, even when charged with a non-custodial offence; the main reason for this is the 'protection of the defendant' (Joseph, 1990); and there is a general tendency to regard the mentally disordered as dangerous (Robertson, 1988). One diversion scheme tries to reduce the time spent on remand in prison by having a psychiatric report completed within one week and therefore a quicker decision of disposal can be arrived at; whether to hospital, the community or the penal system (Banerjee. et al., 1992).

Staite and Martin highlight a number of factors relevant to the concept of diversion; firstly, sometimes magistrates have no choice but to remand in custody; secondly, the pressure of public opinion against persons perceived as dangerous has to be considered; thirdly, reliance on multi-agency co-operation, as no one agency can provide the answer alone; and fourthly, the changes in the shift of emphasis from the criminality to the mental health of mentally disordered offenders is coming from many different sources, places; and the schemes which are in place to identify them vary enormously (Staite and Martin, 1993; Staite, 1994). Boxes 1 and 2 provide some examples of diversion.

Box 1: Allan

Allan had been arrested for breach of the peace. He had spent the night in police custody awaiting appearance in court the following morning. Allan was assessed prior to his appearance by the CPN attached to the court. He was well known to the mental health services but had disengaged with his CPN some three or four months ago. Following discussions between the Crown Prosecution Service, the CPN, social services and the local mental health services it was decided to drop the charges and admit Allan to the local hospital to stabilise his mental state. It was felt by the CPS that it was not in the public interest to pursue the charges and Allan would be better served by treatment by the mental health services. Allan agreed to his admission and was therefore admitted informally to the local psychiatric hospital for treatment.

Box 2: Joe

Joe had been arrested for stabbing a stranger in the street. The stranger was in a critical condition. He had spent the night in police custody. Joe was assessed prior to his court appearance by the visiting CPN and Senior Psychiatric Registrar as the custody sergeant had concerns over his behaviour and thoughts. Joe appeared paranoid and thought-disordered on assessment, and he was out of touch with reality. Joe was not known to the mental health services. Following discussion between the Crown Prosecution Service, defending solicitor, CPN and Senior Registrar it was decided by the Crown Prosecution Service that Joe would have to be charged with the offence of attempted murder. At the Magistrates' court Joe was remanded to prison and a date was set for a crown court hearing. Medical reports were requested and Joe would return back to the Magistrates' court in two weeks. A week later the stranger died in hospital as a result of the injuries received from the stabbing. Joe was brought back to court following the charge of murder, where medical reports were now available, and he was remanded for treatment to a high security hospital under Section 36 of the Mental Health Act 1983. Following appearance at crown court, Joe was ordered to be detained for further treatment under Section 37/41 of the Mental Health Act 1983 at a high security hospital (see Chapter 4 for explanation of these sections of the Mental Health Act 1983).

What the literature says

There is a reasonably large quantity of literature that can be drawn upon in relation to court diversion. Much of this was written around the time that the initial court diversion schemes had developed and these papers often reported on the role of those working in them or the outcomes for those they aimed to serve. In 1994 it was reported that there were over 60 court diversion schemes (Backer-Holst, 1994); however there was little cohesion or systematic approach in their administration. Indeed, whilst some schemes are operational others remained 'paper exercises' (Joseph, 1990). There is no information available in the literature as to how many schemes exist nowadays, yet it is probably safe to say that there will be at least this number in operation.

Gina Hillis described one operational scheme, the Birmingham court diversion scheme, which caters for the largest number of magistrates courts in Europe. The scheme aims to identify the mentally disordered as soon as possible after arrest, offer advice, liaise with other agencies and arrange assessment, treatment and admission if necessary. Assessment is carried out for all offenders who are charged with violent offences, lesser offences committed by those whose behaviour is perceived to be 'odd', and those with a known history of mental disorder. Assessment is in the form of unstructured interview, and looks for the presence of serious disorders, psychosis and depression, potential self-harm and suicide. A high number of the offenders assessed have related problems with substance and alcohol abuse (Hillis, 1993).

Similar operational schemes are described in the literature in Manchester (Holloway and Shaw, 1992; 1993), South East London (Banerjee. et al., 1992; Exworthy and Parrott, 1993), and Inner London (Joseph and Potter, 1990; 1993a; 1993b; James and Hamilton, 1991). Furthermore, all the schemes have access to all the information that the police have, including the previous criminal record of the accused. Some also report that they obtain previous psychiatric and social reports; and discharge summaries from general practitioners and hospitals.

Banerjee et al. (1992) describe a model that integrated psychiatric services for mentally disordered offenders in south east London, where as part of their court liaison service a community psychiatric nurse and a research psychiatrist assessed defendants referred for psychiatric opinion at four magistrates courts. Further developments are discussed as the creation of formal links both inside and outside of the service catchment area, specifically with the community psychiatric nurse developing links with district teams to facilitate community follow-up.

Kennedy and Ward (1992) examined training aspects of a Birmingham based court diversion scheme from a medical perspective. The primary role of the two forensic community mental health nurses was discussed as to undertake initial screening of all prisoners in police custody. The forensic community mental health nurse was described as being able to make recommendations to the court: either, a remand for psychiatric report (bail or custody); or informal admission to the local psychiatric hospital. One year on Gina Hillis (1993), a forensic community mental health nurse in the above scheme, described her own role. This is reported to be equally divided between court diversion work and clinical responsibilities at the local regional secure unit. The nurse's role in the scheme is to identify individuals with a mental illness as soon as possible after arrest and before court appearance; to offer advice to criminal justice agencies to assist in making recommendations to the court; to make arrangements for referral for assessment, treatment and admission if necessary; and to liaise with the court and all other appropriate services. Close liaison takes place with probation officers, solicitors, medical staff and staff from other services, the crown prosecutor, and the forensic community mental health nurse. Gina was clear in stating that although forensic community mental health nurses are unable to make medical diagnoses, nevertheless their in-depth assessments provide the court with presenting symptoms. Moreover, the autonomous nature of the role means they are responsible for making decisions regarding any appropriate courses of action.

The role of two community psychiatric nurses in a project team along with a probation officer and approved social worker in North Humberside are described by Staite (1994). The team members assess prisoners in police custody and court, identifying mentally disordered offenders and consequently arranging packages of care. Close working relationships are reported with the local prison.

Rowlands et al. (1996) demonstrates through their study in Rotherham that diversion schemes can run successfully with a forensic community mental health nurse as the main focus when supervised by a consultant forensic psychiatrist. The role of the forensic community mental health nurse is described as contacting the local police stations at the start of each day and examining the custody records. Each prisoner held in custody overnight is discussed with the custody sergeant, and using a broad, and what is described as over-inclusive, criteria those with possible mental health problems are identified. Other routes of referral are to the forensic community mental health nurse themselves, to probation officers and lawyers. The forensic community mental health nurse undertakes a standard psychiatric history to determine the presence or absence of psychiatric symptoms. Further assessment can be requested from the consultant psychiatrist or senior registrar. The forensic community mental health nurse is said to have established a high profile within the court system, local police and probation services.

Vanderwall (1997) examines his own role as a forensic community mental health nurse based within a remand prison in Bedford. He further describes a second role as operating a court diversion scheme with colleagues in the Luton area. Within the prison he describes the job purpose as threefold: firstly to identify and implement care strategies for mentally disordered offenders; secondly, to offer training and advice to prison staff; and thirdly, to promote effective inter-agency relationships. The role is further conflated into key objectives: to assess the prisoner's mental health needs, plan care or refer to other professionals as necessary; to offer support and counselling; to establish and maintain the service; to liaise with and offer support to the family; establish links with other caring agencies; and to promote good working relationships with prison staff.

Taylor (1998) examining his specific role as a forensic community mental health nurse describes this as ensuring that police, courts, social workers, and mental health services are aware of their own and the role of others, or their potential contribution, in the assessment and treatment of mentally disordered offenders. He informs us that he is in great demand and response has been favourable. Future developments may even include joint assessments with the police surgeon. Finally, Wilkinson (1998) describes the role of the first forensic liaison nurse service in Kent. This service provides nursing input to eleven prisons in the area, where the nurse liaises with prison healthcare staff and the wider multi-disciplinary team. Central to the role is mental health screening and assessment; organising support and follow-up for prisoners with mental health needs on release; and support and education for prison staff. Also encompassed in the role is working within the local court diversion scheme and liaison with the local regional secure unit.

Results that are reported from the schemes in relation to those mentally disordered offenders who are or are not diverted from the prison system, appear to move in the direction of certain trends. Those that are diverted are frequently charged with only minor offences and are first-time offenders. Those that are not diverted tend to be charged with more violent, serious offences and have a history of offending behaviour. However, also included in this group is the minor mentally disordered offender, who is homeless and is often charged with non-custodial offences.

At times, diversion from the criminal justice system to the mental health system has been criticised for being somewhat arbitrary (Davis, 1994), dependent on such factors as the enthusiasm and motivations of individuals concerned with the defendant (i.e. defence or prosecution lawyer, or judge) (Cooke, 1991a); and dominant perceptions of available resources (Exworthy and Parrott, 1993). In reality, it is likely to be a complex interplay of factors which contribute to such decisions and may include professional and personal agendas, media attention, public outcry, aspects of offending behaviour and punishment issues, as well as victim issues. In any event, reputations of courts, judges, lawyers, and indeed, psychiatrists seem to be a reasonable prediction of diversion into one system rather than another. Furthermore, this prediction pivots on the perceived level of compassion exercised in relation to the mentally disordered offender which can vacillate in response to sensational crimes which outrage the general public.

Certainly court diversion schemes have been criticised on the grounds that they are not in the public's interest and that they are violations of the rights of the offender by exerting undue pressure to comply with psychiatric treatment (McKittrick and Eysenck, 1984). Furthermore, it should be asked – to what extent should mentally disordered offenders be held responsible for their actions; and how much consideration should be given to the views of the victim (Prins, 1992)? Indeed, the formal legal process can be a valuable way of testing a mentally disordered offenders' concept of reality (Smith and Donovan, 1990). Defenders of such statements argue that: diversion should be justified on humanitarian factors and not economic factors (Cooke, 1991a); if an offence is more likely to be linked to mental disorder than greed, badness or wickedness, then diversion might possibly be the more humane action to take (Moody, 1993); and schemes need to aim towards obtaining a delicate balance between public interest, the rights of the accused, and clinical effectiveness (Cooke, 1991b). Notwithstanding the above criticisms court diversion schemes are morally fashionable, as they are, theoretically, an attempt to ensure that the mentally disordered offenders are more appropriately ensconced within the perceived treatment system rather than a punitive one (Richer 1990).

Policy

We have already seen above that current government policy allows for the early detection of mental disorder in those that have offended; and that wherever possible individuals should be diverted into the mental health care system. The Crown Prosecution Service (CPS) provides information on their website about the decision to prosecute mentally disordered offenders including the principle, guidance and procedure:

- **Procedure includes**: the importance of three key documents: the Code for Crown Prosecutors (the Code); the Home Office Circular 66/90 – Provision for Mentally Disordered Offenders; and the Home Office Circular 12/95 – Mentally Disordered Offenders: Inter Agency Working. Also the importance of taking into account medical reports.
- **Guidance includes**: the definition of mental disorder; how admissible are the confessions of the mentally disordered offenders; issues of diversion

and public interest; and the standard and form of information that is required to establish mental disorder.

- **Procedure includes**: the relationship between agencies; the Criminal Procedure (Insanity and Unfitness to Plead) Act 1991; and the Mental Health Act 1983.

Conclusions

Diversion from the criminal justice system to mental health services is certainly not a practice of the past. In current government legalisation it can only be set to grow. For diversion to be successful it needs to be interdisciplinary in its approach and have the mentally disordered person at its centre rather than the system that serves it. That is to say that the system should be in place to serve the needs of those who need to access it. This requires a well planned and collaborative approach, but above all the funds to run such systems. In summary:

- Diversion can occur in a number of ways, either following arrest, from Magistrates' court, following remand into custody, at sentencing, or following a custodial sentence.
- The point at which diversion occurs depends largely on whether the Crown Prosecution Service is prepared to discontinue criminal proceedings.
- In the case of the more serious, violent mentally disordered offender, it is almost inevitable that they will spend a period in custody either awaiting a psychiatric report, or transfer for further assessment or treatment.
- Most of the literature on diversion indicates that scheme workers aim to identify mentally disordered people as soon as possible after arrest, offer advice, liaise with other agencies and arrange assessment, treatment and admission if necessary.
- At times diversion from the criminal justice system to the mental health system has been criticised for being somewhat arbitrary and dependent on such factors as: the enthusiasm and motivations of individuals concerned with the defendant.

References

Backer-Holst, T. (1994) A new window of opportunity: the implications of the Reed Report for psychiatric care. *Psychiatric Care*. 1: 1, 15–8.

Banerjee, S., Exworthy, T., O'Neill-Byrne, K. and Parrott, J. (1992) An integrated service for mentally disordered offenders. *Psychiatric Bulletin*. 16: 773–5.

Cooke, D.J. (1991a) Psychological treatment as an alternative to prosecution: a form of primary diversion. *The Howard Journal*. 30: 1, 53–65.

Cooke, D.J. (1991b) Treatment as an alternative to prosecution: offenders diverted for treatment. *British Journal of Psychiatry*. 158: 785–91.

Crown Prosecution Service (2004) *Legal Guidance: Decision to Prosecute: Mentally Disordered Offenders http://www.cps.gov.uk/legal/section3/chapter_a.html* [online] [27th July 2004].

Davis, S. (1994) Factors associated with the diversion of mentally disordered offenders. *Bulletin of the American Academy of Psychiatry and Law*. 22: 3, 389–97.

DoH and Home Office (1993) *Review of Health and Social Services for Mentally Disordered Offenders and Others Requiring Similar Services, Volume 2 Service Needs*. London: HMSO.

Exworthy, T., Parrott, J. (1993) Evaluation of a diversion from custody scheme at Magistrates' courts. *Journal of Forensic Psychiatry*. 4: 3, 497–505.

Hillis, G. (1993) Diverting tactics. *Nursing Times*. 89: 1, 24–7.

Hillis, G. (1999) Diverting people with mental health problems from the criminal justice system. In Tarbuck, P., Topping-Morris, B.and Burnard, P. (Eds.) *Forensic Mental Health Nursing: Strategy and Implementation*. London: Whurr.

Holloway, J. and Shaw, J. (1992) Providing a forensic psychiatry service to a Magistrates' court. *Journal of Forensic Psychiatry*. 3: 1,153–9.

Holloway, J. and Shaw, J. (1993) Providing a forensic psychiatry service to a Magistrates' court: a follow-up study. *Journal of Forensic Psychiatry*. 4: 3, 575–81.

Home Office (1990) *Provision for Mentally Disordered Offenders. Circular 66/90*. London: Home Office.

James, D.V. and Hamilton, L.W. (1991) The Clerkenwell Scheme: assessing efficacy and cost of a psychiatric liaison service to a Magistrates' court. *British Medical Journal*. 303: 282–5.

Joseph, P.L. (1990) Mentally disordered offenders: diversion from the criminal justice system. *Journal of Forensic Psychiatry*. 1: 2, 133–8.

Joseph, P.L. and Potter, M. (1990) Mentally disordered homeless offenders: diversion from custody. *Health Trends*. 22: 2, 51–3.

Joseph, P.L. and Potter, M. (1993a) Diversion from custody I: psychiatric assessment at the Magistrates' court. *British Journal of Psychiatry*. 162: 325–30.

Joseph, P.L. and Potter, M. (1993b) Diversion from custody II: Effect on hospital and prison resources. *British Journal of Psychiatry*. 162: 330–4.

Kennedy, N.M. and Ward, M. (1992) Training aspects of the Birmingham Court Diversion Scheme. *Psychiatric Bulletin*. 16: 630–1.

McKittrick, N. and Eysenck, S. (1984) Diversion: a big fix? *Justice of the Peace*. June 16: 377–9: 393–4.

Moody, S. (1983) *Diversion from the Criminal Justice Process*. Edinburgh: Scottish Office Central Research Unit.

Phipps, A.J. (1994) The Reed Report: mentally disordered offenders. *Prison Service Journal*. 95: 50–2.

Prins, H. (1992) The diversion of the mentally disordered: some problems for criminal justice, penology and health care. *Journal of Forensic Psychiatry*. 3: 3, 431–43.

Richer, A.D. (1990) Should the prison medical service develop its role in the treatment of mentally ill offenders. *Prison Service Journal*. 81: 15–8.

Robertson, G. (1988) Arrest patterns among mentally disordered offenders. *British Journal of Psychiatry*. 153: 313–6.

Robertson, G., Dell, S., James, K. and Grounds, A. (1994) Psychotic men remanded in custody to Brixton Prison. *British Journal of Psychiatry*. 164: 55–61.

Rowlands, R., Inch, H., Rodger, W. and Soliman, A. (1996) Diverted to where? what happens to the diverted mentally disordered offender. *The Journal of Forensic Psychiatry*. 7: 2, 284–96.

Smith, J. and Donovan, N. (1990) The prosecution of psychiatric inpatients. *Journal of Forensic Psychiatry*. 1: 379–83.

Staite, C. (1994) Diversion from custody for mentally disordered offenders. *Prison Service Journal*. 95: 42–5.

Staite, C. and Martin, N. (1993) What else can we do? new initiatives in diversion from custody. *Justice of the Peace*. 157: 280–1.

Taylor, S. (1998) Helping with enquiries. *Mental Health Nursing*. 18: 1, 26–7.

Vanderwall, C. (1997) The role of the community forensic mental health nurse: initiatives for cross agency work. *Psychiatric Care*. 4: 6, 283–6.

Wilkinson, L. (1998) Liaison service provides safety network. *Nursing Times*. 94: 37.

Further Reading

Hillis, G. (1999) Diverting people with mental health problems from the criminal justice system. In Tarbuck, P., Topping-Morris, B. and Burnard, P. (Eds.) *Forensic Mental Health Nursing: Strategy and Implementation*. London: Whurr, Chapter 4, 36–50.

Hillis, G. (2000) Diversion from the criminal justice system. In: Chaloner, C. and Coffey, M. (Eds.) *Forensic Mental Health Nursing: Current Approaches*. Oxford: Blackwell Science.

Chapter 9

Risk Assessment and Compliance in Probation and Mental Health Practice

Rob Canton

Introduction

Protecting the Public heads the list of aims of the National Probation Service in its original strategic framework, where the first 'stretch objective' concerns the assessment and management of risk and dangerousness (National Probation Service, 2001). The ascendancy of risk in contemporary probation practice has to be understood in the context of a culture of control where public protection 'has become the dominant theme of penal policy' (Garland, 2001; Loader and Sparks, 2002). Garland draws attention to the change in emotional tone of crime policy which now substitutes for the welfarist image of the offender as a 'disadvantaged, deserving, subject of need' the 'stereotypical depictions of unruly youth, dangerous predators, and incorrigible career criminals' (2001).

In mental health policy, too, fear has become a determining influence on the character of the psychiatric system (Laurance, 2003). The position of mentally disturbed people is inevitably precarious in a society that gives such prominence to risk (Prins, 1999; Busfield, 2002). A British survey in 2000 showed that negative attitudes towards mentally disturbed people are widespread – not least ideas of being a danger to others and unpredictable (Crisp et al., 2000) – a distortion to which the media continue to make a significant contribution (Philo, 1996). Where prediction and knowledge are needed to manage our risks, what is to be made of risks that seem inherently unknowable and unpredictable?

The vocabulary of madness is readily invoked in reaction to dreadful acts and then whoever did this must be mad is turned into this is the sort of thing that mad people do (Busfield, 2002). Porter refers to this as a:

. . . demonising process . . . psychologically and anthropologically driven, arising out of deep-seated and perhaps unconscious needs to order the world by demarcating self from others . . . [which] reinforces our fragile sense of self-identity and self-worth through the pathologisation of pariahs.

(Porter, 2002)

This chapter explores the processes of risk assessment in probation and mental health practice. It considers the association between mental disturbance and crime and looks at some methods used to assess risk. It touches upon the opportunities and challenges of inter-agency work. The chapter concludes by arguing that while risk assessment has an indispensable role in both probation and psychiatry it can distort practice and, by estranging those at the centre of risk management, increase levels of risk.

Mental disorder and crime

The relationship between mental disorder and offending is complex. As Prins points out:

. . . it is hardly surprising that we experience difficulty in trying to establish connections between these two somewhat ill-defined and complex behaviours.

(Prins, 1995)

There is, however, some evidence to suggest that certain kinds of mental disturbance do make offending – especially violent offending – more likely, although this increased risk does not apply to most kinds of mental disorder (see Blumenthal and Lavender, 2001; Busfield, 2002). In her recent review, Hodgins concludes that:

Persons who develop major mental disorders are more likely than persons with no mental disorders to be convicted of criminal offences.

(Hodgins, 2004)

She also rejects the suggestion that discrimination against them can explain this. Any correlation cannot be assumed to be causal, however. Moore insists that:

It is not sufficient to ask whether the client suffers from a mental illness . . . most of the actions of a mentally ill person are a result of non-illness factors.

(Moore, 1996)

It will always be relevant to ask whether illness was a sufficient, necessary or significant part of the motivational drive or a disinhibiting factor (Moore, 1996). An imputation of mental disturbance, however, typically closes down an exploration of reason or motive: madness is the cause of the conduct.

Reasons are not to be found – indeed not to be looked for – because these are people who are not reasonable or rational (Canton, 1995). In reality, of course, mentally disturbed people behave for the same range of reasons as everyone else.

In practice, this has serious consequences for risk assessment. Unless psychiatric and criminogenic factors are carefully disentangled, stability or improvement in a psychiatric condition could mislead a risk assessor into overlooking an increase in the level of risk. Conversely, where the mental illness *is* causally influential, early identification of symptoms and 'falling out of care' may be singularly important (Moore, 1996; Prins, 1999). As Skeem and Mulvey state:

> . . . *a patient's primary treatment goals may assume a much different focus if (a) a deterioration in the quality of his interpersonal relationships is followed by an exacerbation of his psychotic symptoms, and then violence; than if (b) an exacerbation of his psychotic symptoms is followed by a deterioration in his relationships, which then leads to violence.*
> (Skeem and Mulvey, 2002)

Peay investigates the historical origins of psychiatry's claim to 'expertise in the identification and prediction of dangerousness' (Peay, 1982). The claim to this authority is the more doubtful when it is clear that criminal predictors 'outperform' diagnostic ones – that the risk factors for mentally disordered offenders are substantially the same as for other offenders (Bonta et al., 1998). The meta-analysis by Bonta and colleagues demonstrated that this was true, both for general and violent forms of recidivism. Indeed, the presence of mental illness indicated *less* recidivism (Bonta et al., 1998).

In their authoritative overview of *Violence and Mental Disorder*, Blumenthal and Lavender tentatively propose that some 'symptom profiles' – especially violent thoughts and delusions, threat/control over-ride symptoms (feeling of being dominated by some outside force) – might lead to violence and are certainly better indicators of risk than a diagnostic label itself (Blumenthal and Lavender, 2001). They conclude more confidently that:

> *The mentally ill make a very small contribution to violence in society . . . Focusing on the mentally disordered tends to obscure other important causes of violence . . . The overall risk of violence posed by individuals with mental disorder is low, while their needs are substantial.*
> (Blumenthal and Lavender, 2001)

Aspects of assessment

Developments in risk assessment in criminal justice and in psychiatry have followed a similar trajectory – at least partly because of the increasing influence of forensic psychology in the understanding of offending behaviour.

A conventional distinction is between clinical and actuarial assessment. Clinical assessment relies on the practitioner's skills, experience and diagnostic judgement. Clinical has strong medical connotations, betraying its provenance in the discourse of psychiatric medicine. Probation officers, while never clinicians, have used this method for most of the history of the Service. A more generic term for the approach would be person-by-person assessment. Since research was said to have demonstrated that clinical risk assessment was unreliable, the 'second generation' of assessment methods established empirical correlations between risk markers and the target behaviour. Brown warns against the assumption, implicit in the metaphor of generations, that this is a linear progress. These approaches should rather be seen as 'differences in the underlying conception of what can be held to constitute risk' (2000). The subject of this actuarial assessment is compared with the relevantly matched group to yield a probability estimate – typically a percentage score or assignment to a risk category (see, for example, Brown, 2000; Dolan and Doyle, 2000; Blumenthal and Lavender, 2001; Kemshall, 2001, 2003).

While the product of an actuarial risk assessment is often referred to as a prediction, it is better understood as a probability statement. There is no event that an actuarial risk assessment predicts. A prediction is confirmed or falsified by future events, but the truth value of a probability statement depends rather on the soundness of the probability calculation. This explains the paradox to which Moore draws attention: 'successful prediction should actually lead to prevention, and thus prove itself wrong' (Moore, 1996).

Whatever it describes, predicts or weighs, the risk assessment *assigns individuals to categories* – an act of ascription as much as description (Peay, 1982). On the other hand, no contemporary service can be entirely demand-led. Kemshall gives an example of a screening instrument that identified unmanageably large numbers of high risk individuals, so that the thresholds had to be revised, and astutely concludes that: 'In effect, the availability (or perceived availability) of resources determines the risk categorisation' (Kemshall, 2003).

The best established correlates of reconviction are criminal history variables (Bonta et al., 1998), which of course cannot be changed. Skeem and Mulvey (2002) usefully distinguish between risk markers – correlates that are not (or are not known to be) causally related to the behaviour – and risk factors – considerations that *are* causally linked. In these terms, historically grounded actuarial assessment identifies markers rather than factors.

Actuarial assessments, then, uncouple risk assessment from its management. As Moore explains:

Because the sound assessment of risk will be based on the formulation of the mechanisms underlying the behaviour, it will automatically identify

*those processes which appear to be key elements in increasing or reducing
such risk.*

(Moore, 1996)

This is something that most actuarial instruments conspicuously fail to do. In a particular case, they may assign a probability – they may show a person to be a member of a population with (say) a relatively high base rate of reconviction – but they give no guidance about how to influence things.

To overcome clinical unreliability and actuarial irrelevance, a third generation of instruments has been developed that introduce 'dynamic' risk factors – contemporary and at least potentially amenable to change – that might guide intervention and evaluate progress (Dolan and Doyle, 2000; Robinson, 2003; Raynor, 2002; Kemshall, 2003). Skeem and Mulvey suggest, incidentally, that the conventional dichotomy between static and dynamic factors is better seen as a continuum with some markers absolutely unchangeable, some changing apace and others somewhere in between. They conclude that: 'Conceptualising the degree of malleability of risk factors may be crucial in planning risk assessment strategies' (2002).

All historical markers, however, are static and it is these that seem to have the strongest correlations with general and violent recidivism (Bonta et al., 1998; Dolan and Doyle, 2000).

There remain the challenges of instantiation: there is still a need to make a judgement, person by person, to determine whether the risk factor is present (an inescapably clinical element in any actuarial scheme). For example, if *stress* is an established risk factor, there is still the question of deciding if the individual is in fact under stress. As Busfield (2002) notes, such judgements are likely to play a more significant part in assessment as instruments become more sophisticated. She further cautions against expecting too much of actuarial instruments – partly because of the familiar problem of trying to predict rare events – but also because:

*. . . the factors that predict one type of violence are not the same as those
that predict others. Consequently, it is very difficult to develop measures of
risk assessment that are sufficiently flexible to encompass the prediction of
the diverse types of violence that can occur . . . and related to this, violence
is frequently circumstantial: the capacity to predict violence is likely to be
limited by the fact that whether an individual is violent or not will depend
on a range of circumstances and contingencies, on a particular constella-
tion of events that are themselves hard to predict.*

(Busfield, 2002)

A promising approach is sometimes referred to as anamnestic (from the Greek, a *calling to mind* or *remembering*). This involves an analysis of the circumstances in which the individual has offended in the past and an attempt to anticipate *and to manage* these circumstances in the future (Brown, 2000; McGuire, 2002; Skeem and Mulvey, 2002). The recognition and relevance of these factors should be actuarially supported. This painstaking and thorough approach (see also Scott, 1977; Potts, 1995; Moore, 1996; Prins, 1999) yields neither a prediction nor a probability estimate, but *conditional* propositions – '*If* these specified circumstances obtain, violence is more likely . . .', '*Unless* this safeguard is in place . . .' – which may be specific, amenable to influence and sustained by empirically validated correlations.

Information in risk assessment

All these approaches depend upon the availability and intelligent interpreta-tion of reliable information and this, notoriously, cannot be assumed. Morgan (2000) conveniently identifies several sources of information and these are set out in the table below, together with my own comments.

Sources	Comment
Access to past records.	Variable. Not always shared between agencies (Prins, 1999). Even relatively 'straightforward' information about previous convictions may not be reliable and can be very differently interpreted (Stephens and Brown, 2001).
Self-report at interview.	An invaluable resource that can be devalued. 'Many calculations of risk are inevitably made at a crisis point in the management of the case and therefore in the life of the client, who has everything to lose and so strongly motivated to present themselves as a non-harmful. They are frequently disbelieved as a result' (Moore, 1996). It can also be 'closed off' unless some degree of trust can be established (see discussion on compliance below).
Observing discrepancies between verbal and non-verbal cues.	May be indicative of mental illness, but may occur for other reasons too and is highly 'culture bound' (Rack, 1982; Fernando, Ndegwa and Wilson, 1998; Bhui, 1999).

Reports from significant others: • Carers, friends, relatives • Other team members • Other mental health agencies • CJ agencies	Carers and friends may be inhibited by different sorts of fears and anxieties (Moore, 1996), but their information may be invaluable – if often under-appreciated (Scott, 1997; Prins, 1999). Claims about confidentiality may interfere with information exchange between agencies (Prins, 1999; McGuire, 2002). Note that some – even serious – incidents of actual violence may be unrecorded (or inaccessible), perhaps because they took place in hospital and were dealt with without police involvement (Crichton, 1995; 1996). Attempts at violence may have been frustrated and so unreported (Ritchie et al., 1994). Exchange of information and collaboration in risk assessment and management also depends on a sufficiently common vocabulary and set of concepts between disciplines and organisations.
Rating scales or descriptive narrative reports.	A feature of both actuarial and anamnestic assessment (see the text).
Intuitive gut reactions ('vital clues, not easily documented' Morgan, 2000).	But again culture-bound and a potential source of discrimination unless scrutinised and validated. Clinical assessment is likely to be vulnerable to this, although it should not be overlooked that actuarialism, if not properly cross-checked for its applicability to different populations, can institutionalise unfairness.
Recognising repeated patterns of behaviour.	The essence of sound anamnestic assessment (see the text).

Risk assessment in probation practice

The emergence of risk to its present salience in probation practice has been thoroughly discussed elsewhere (Kemshall 2000; 2003; Robinson, 2001; 2003; Bhui, 2002; Oldfield, 2002). Formal risk assessment has become a routine activity for probation staff. The outcome of this assessment, whatever it may *disclose* about an individual offender, is a principal determinant of the nature and level of service they will receive. (For example eligibility for most accredited programmes is determined by an Offender Group Reconviction Score within a specified range.)

A full review of the actuarial instruments used in probation and psychiatry is beyond the scope of the chapter. Any such review would need to discuss (at least) the SACJ and Matrix 2000 for sex offenders and the *iterative classification tree* (Monahan et al., 2000). For description and critical discussion, see Kemshall (2001; 2003), Dolan and Doyle (2000), Raynor et al. (2000), Blumenthal and Lavender (2001.) However, the widely used Offender Group Reconviction Score (OGRS) is an example of a second generational instrument which depends solely on static risk markers (rather than factors – see above). It generates reliable assessment for groups, but offers little guidance to practitioners in the individual case. An individual's score is a probability estimate of reconviction (a proxy for re-offending, even if the best proxy there is) within two years. OGRS does not attempt to predict the *nature* of the offending which will lead to this reconviction and, since the risk factors for different behaviours are themselves so different (Moore, 1996), can make a very limited contribution to risk management.

The development of instruments to assess risk or need is an attempt to create 'third generation' methods which, by identifying dynamic risk factors (those that can change and are at least potentially amenable to influence), can inform a risk management plan and help to measure progress (Raynor et al., 2000; Robinson, 2003; Kemshall, 2001; 2003). The Offender Assessment System (OASys) is an attempt to consolidate the best features of its predecessors – the Level of Service Inventory – Revised (LSI-R) and Assessment Case Management and Evaluation (ACE) (on which, see Raynor et al., 2000). OASys was developed jointly by the Probation and Prison Services, and while this must be seen in the context of broader political aspirations to strengthen connections between prison and probation, it is of particular interest for its attempt to construct a common set of concepts, a shared vocabulary in which practitioners from different professional backgrounds can discuss risk.

The policy aspiration, then, is that probation staff apply validated assessment instruments and that these structured assessments inform their risk management strategies. The position, however, is likely to be much more complicated than this. Cohen famously warned against mistaking the 'story' for the practice (Cohen, 1985) and there are a number of studies showing that the implementation of avowed policy is far from straightforward (Lynch, 2000; Kemshall and Maguire, 2001; Robinson, 2001). Thus, Robinson (2001) discovered that actuarial approaches in probation are understood and implemented variably and that staff continue to fall back on 'clinical' approaches, especially in higher risk cases:

Between policy and practice stand the interpretation and mediation of policies by operational managers, required to balance and implement competing demands within limited resources [and] . . . *by frontline workers operating within well-established working practices, ideologies and value bases.*

(Kemshall, 2003)

These influences mediate policy implementation: they do not block it. The upshot can be anything between a complete shutting out of the policy and its fulfilment as intended, but is most likely to lead to a qualified – and, as it may be, distorted – implementation. Again, although those processes may be described as resistance, it would be a mistake to see this as obduracy or as a deliberate unwillingness to change. It may be better seen as a collision, when the carefully wrought criteria of policy encounter the complexity and vicissitudes of real life.

There are also cultural tensions, which, while almost certain to be found in inter-agency practice (Maguire et al., 2001), can as well occur within a profession. Many probation officers are uncomfortable with the pre-eminence of public protection within the discourse of their profession (Robinson, 2001) and that needs are now reinscribed as risk factors (compare Hannah-Moffat, 1999).

It is important too not to overlook the circumstances in which assessments are undertaken. As Moore points out:

Many calculations of risk are inevitably made at a crisis point in the management of the case and therefore in the life of the client . . .

(Moore, 1996)

when levels of anxiety are high. Even a structured assessment involves negotiation when it is properly shared with the service user.

There is again the question of instantiation. A key insight of cognitive behavioural psychology is its recognition that people interpret their experiences:

Cognitive-behavioural approaches emphasise the key role played . . . by the appraisal of events. The latter takes place at a cognitive level. Individuals' perceptions and constructions of an event influence their emotional and behavioural reactions to it and so determine the coping processes called into play for dealing with it. There are obviously some events, such as serious illness or injury, which are likely to be found stressful by most people. But there are numerous events which, appraised differently by two individuals, can have diametrically opposite effects on them. While one feels almost no reaction at all and experiences little or no stress, the other may be overwhelmed.

(McGuire, 2001)

Some actuarial approaches can find no place for expressions of intent, interpretations or meanings with which offenders invest their behaviour. Yet *meanings* are crucially important to risk assessment. As Moore says:

> As in so many other areas of the assessment . . . it is the individual's reaction in the past to their long-term conditions which is significant, not the apparent abnormality of the conditions nor the extent to which they would unsettle the average person.
>
> (Moore, 1996; Prins, 1999)

These meanings and nuances can often only be understood after considerable discussion and there is at least a possibility that actuarial assessment, in its haste to identify objective risk markers, discourages this exploration.

Assessment of the risk of violence to others in psychology and psychiatry

Many of these considerations, of course, also apply to assessment in the mental health professions. Here too the assessment and management of risk of violence to others have become central to professional practice, with considerable implications for forensic services (Prins, 1999; Jewesbury and McCulloch, 2002).

Dolan and Doyle (2000) review unaided clinical risk assessment and cite studies that suggest that, after all, 'clinicians may be better than was believed.' (that is to say, at the time of the initial challenges to their reliability). However that may be, this scepticism gave an impetus to the development of actuarial instruments of which one of the best known is the Violence Risk Assessment Guide (VRAG). This is a 'second generation' instrument, based on static factors, which could be said to be a counterpart to the criminological OGRS and, like OGRS, cannot encompass 'the nature, severity, frequency and imminence' of future violence (Cooke, 2000).

This limited potential to contribute to risk management is no doubt part of the reason why actuarial instruments:

> . . . remain primarily research instruments which are largely ignored by clinicians.
>
> (Blumenthal and Lavender, 2001)

The 'third generation' of structured clinical judgement attempts to combine the empirical soundness offered by well-grounded actuarial approaches with the flexibility and individualisation of the best clinical practice. One of the best known of these instruments is the Historical/Clinical/Risk Management 20 item scale (HCR–20). This combines 10 historical items (some of which, incidentally, do not appear to be particularly static – for example, *employment problems* and *relationship stability*) with five clinical items and five risk management ones. Dolan and Doyle report that the H-items show stronger correlations with violence than the C-scales (2000; Cooke, 2000).

Much of the research in this area is prescriptive – saying how psychiatrists ought to go about assessing risk – rather than descriptive of how this is actually accomplished (Skeem and Mulvey, 2002). Policy implementation is mediated here too of course. Skeem and Mulvey plausibly speculate that, rather than mechanistically applying actuarially grounded risk criteria, clinicians are more likely to:

> . . . assess basic risk factors that they believe are critical in most cases (e.g. age, gender, violence history) and risk factors they believe are important to the specific case . . . They might then, for example, intuitively compare the extent to which the [Mentally Disordered Offenders (MDOs)] characteristics matched those of their prototypes of violent offenders . . . As the number of features that the MDO shared with their prototype of a violent offender . . . increased, so would the likelihood that the MDO would be deemed potentially violent.
>
> (Skeem and Mulvey, 2002)

Personality disorder and psychopathy

One of the best validated psychological assessment instruments is the Hare Psychopathy Checklist – Revised (PCL-R). Its reliability in 'predicting' violence has led to its incorporation into other instruments: VRAG and HCR-20 include a PCL-R score as a risk marker. Twenty items are rated in three categories: inter-personal/affective, social deviance, additional items (for further description and discussion, see Kemshall, 2001). Although most of the items have an ordinary language meaning – *glibness, lack of remorse or guilt, irresponsibility* – they are given a precise clinical meaning that enables a high degree of inter-rater reliability to be achieved.

A use that PCL-R has in criminal justice is to identify those who would be unlikely to be able to benefit from conventional accredited programmes (Clark, 2003). Moore (1996) gives an example of the counter-productive consequences of enhancing victim empathy where causing pain to the victim is a central element of the motivation.

Psychopathy, which does not appear in the psychiatric diagnostic manuals, overlaps significantly with anti-social personality disorder (ASPD). All PCL-R psychopaths meet the criteria for ASPD, though fewer than one-third of ASPD are PCL-R psychopaths (Hodgins and Müller-Isberner, 2000). An additional layer of complication is that neither group is co-extensive with legal psychopaths (i.e. psychopathic within the meaning of the Mental Health Act, 1983, s. 1 [2]), with whom those with *borderline personality disorder* also significantly overlap. ASPD was one of the few clinical factors which correlated with reconviction in Bonta's meta-analysis. Within the prison population, nearly half of all sentenced male prisoners could be assessed with ASPD (for references and discussion, Canton, 2002).

There seems significant conceptual uncertainty in the terminology of psychopathy and personality disorder (Tyrer, 2000; Blackburn, 2000) and the potential for even more confusion in inter-agency exchanges concerning:

- The meanings of the terms.
- The extent to which they *explain* – as opposed to describe – offending behaviour (compare Prins, 1999; Busfield, 2002. As Prins says, it is true by *definition* that people designated as psychopaths present an increased risk to others (1999).)
- The extent to which the instruments identify factors or markers (see above for this distinction).
- The extent to which these markers or factors are amenable to change.

These latter two points are, as ever, crucial, because what the practitioner needs is not prediction, but guidance about scope for effective intervention.

Assessment of other risks

Even more acutely than in the probation service, perhaps, mental health practitioners – psychologists, nurses and psychiatrists – may feel an unease at the prominence given to the assessment and management of the risk of violence to others that their patients pose. The 'double mandate' (Hodgins and Müller-Isberner, 2000) – to treat as well as to prevent crime – may be distorted. Crowe and Carlyle conclude that:

> The mental health nursing profession needs to carefully examine its socially mandated role as guardians of those who pose a risk to others to ensure that its practise represents its espoused therapeutic responsibilities.

(Crowe and Carlyle, 2003)

As Mullen writes:

> Surely it is obvious that the chances of a mentally disordered person acting violently should be carefully evaluated and every step taken to prevent such a consequence. It is, perhaps, not quite as obvious that a central, if not the primary, responsibility of a mental health professional is to the wider community rather than their patient. It is not entirely obvious how a responsibility to predict risk is to be discharged. It is certainly not obvious how a clinician should act if they do suspect their patient is more probable to act violently. And finally, it is far from obvious that we should allow concerns about the risk which some of our patients may present to others to become a major determinant of our approach to all our patients.

(Mullen, 2002)

In the UK, this debate has taken a sharp turn with the anticipated Dangerous and Severe Personality Disorder Programme which anticipates at least the possibility that some people may be detained in psychiatric facilities even where there is no anticipated therapeutic benefit (Department of Health and Home Office, 2000b).

Meanwhile, Munro and Rumgay point to the limitations of improved risk assessment in reducing homicide and conclude that:

More homicides could be prevented by good mental healthcare which detected relapse earlier than would be averted by attempts at better risk assessment and management.

(Munro and Rumgay, 2000)

This is a further reminder that undue emphasis on risk assessment can distort the quality of care with consequences that could be called ironic were they not tragic (Munro and Rumgay, 2001). The over-prediction of risk is always likely (Moore, 1996; Busfield, 2002; Laurance, 2003) and among the consequences that may follow are estrangement and the avoidance of services.

As Laurance cogently argues, risks to mentally disturbed people are much more securely established by research findings than are the risks that they present to others. The increased risk of suicide is reasonably well known:

Approximately one quarter of suicides in England and Wales, Scotland and Northern Ireland had been in contact with mental health services in the year before death; this represents around 1,500 cases per year . . . Mental health teams in England and Wales regarded 22 per cent of the suicides as preventable . . . but around three-quarters identified factors that could have reduced risk, mainly improved patient compliance and closer supervision.

(National Confidential Inquiry, 2001)

Less familiar, perhaps, is the finding that mentally ill people are six times more likely to be murdered than the general population (Hiroeh et al., 2001). They are also at significantly more risk of becoming victims of violence – and indeed of fatal accident.

Even if the assessment of a risk of violence to others is an important part of contemporary psychiatric practice, it is assuredly not the only risk assessment to be undertaken. Morgan (2000), for example, lists risks of self-harm or suicide, of neglect and of a variety of 'other risks' apart from crime-related considerations. The therapeutic relationship depends on due regard for the well-being of the patient and, if this is distorted by a preoccupation with risk of violence to others, effective engagement will be that much harder to achieve.

Inter-disciplinary practice

Moore notes that:

> *One of the most common weaknesses identified in risk assessment is the tendency for it to be carried out by single disciplines, or even individuals. The range of information necessary is rarely to be found within the training and expertise of one profession, and predictive accuracy is likely to be compromised as a result.*

(1996; compare Prins, 1999)

Yet inter-agency work notoriously presents challenges, as well as opportunities (Maguire et al., 2001; McGuire, 2002; Rumgay, 2003). Whenever representatives from different organisations deliberate about particular cases, the influences shown in the diagram below will shape their negotiations:

This basic diagram illustrates some of the influences that guide the taking of decisions. The identified influences are applied to the *facts of the case* and a decision is taken, the implementation of which is again mediated by these influences. (A fuller account would explore the interactions, subtle and complex, among these influences.) It is most important to note that the *facts*

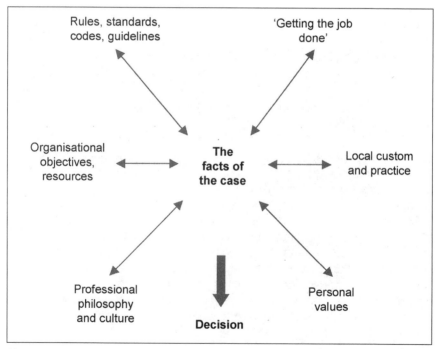

Figure 2

of the case, so far from being self-evident and independent, are *constructed* within the framework of these influences (compare McConville, Sanders and Leng, 1991). Although this analysis can illuminate decision-taking within a single agency, it particularly highlights some of the challenges of inter-agency decision-taking. Different organisations, 'multiple organisations with diverse goals', (McGuire, 2002), will bring profoundly different perspectives to their shared endeavours. McGuire identifies four particular aspects of difference:

> *The first derives from the theoretical models and empirical bases of the disciplines involved. The second arises in the application of these models within a legal context. The third relates to the manner of training of the multifarious practitioner groups which, some directly, others more tangentially, play a part in this field. The fourth relates to organisational aspects of service provision in a multi-agency context.*
>
> (McGuire, 2002)

There are also formal and informal differences of power (Rumgay, 2003).

Maguire and Kemshall have explored how cultural tensions may be acted out in Multi-Agency Public Protection Panels, which consider plans of supervision and inter-agency working with high risk and dangerous offenders (Maguire et al., 2001; Kemshall and Maguire, 2001). Probation officers sometimes felt a strain in being expected to set aside traditional occupational priorities like rehabilitation and this is likely to be a still sharper dilemma for health care professionals (see above), who do not routinely participate in all such panels.

It is not argued here that these differences necessarily impair inter-agency work, only that they are considerations which inter-agency work needs to take into account. Criminal justice and mental health agencies will bring their respective assessment instruments to their negotiations – conspicuously, for sex offenders, the Structured Anchored Clinical Judgement tool and its successor Matrix 2000 – but often revert to clinical and 'common sense' assessments (Kemshall and Maguire, 2001). This is more than ever likely in the hardest cases, where the failure of assessment instruments, even third generation ones, to provide the information needed – about the type of offence, its specific risk factors, its imminence, what can be done to prevent it and so on – will push practitioners back on the invaluable but variable resources of experience, good sense and sound judgement.

Developing Bonta's insight – that criminal history and other factors 'predict' more reliably than mental health factors – McGuire anticipates a possibility that the psychological violence risk assessment instruments could be progressively assimilated into general re-offending risk tools (McGuire, 2002; reference there cited). This would enhance the development of a common vocabulary among different professions, but there would remain the persistent challenge of what to do with the 'prediction' arrived at. As Mullen notes:

> *The individual's current risk status may be influenced by static and abiding characteristics of the individual but will be best predicted by understanding the dynamics of the ever-changing interactions between the individual's vulnerabilities and the environment. This process seems to require at least a partial rehabilitation of the derived clinical approach.*

(Mullen, 2002)

Mullen concludes that the therapeutic role of psychiatry must be reaffirmed against the powerful momentum of the priority of public protection. Although the case can be made on ethical grounds, there are also reasons to think that this difference of aspect could constitute better public protection.

Risk assessment, coercion and compliance

The contemporary Probation Service emphasises the importance of rigorous enforcement practice (see Hedderman, 2003). Laurance (2003) describes the increasingly coercive character of psychiatric service. But in both areas, there are powerful emerging arguments that coercion is not only ethically dubious but practically self-defeating. Grounds puts it well:

> *Supervision is not primarily a surveillance and crime control process, but a framework of support. Monitoring depends centrally on the maintenance of a relationship with the patient, with every effort being made to achieve co-operation, openness and trust. Surveillance that is onerous and outside a framework of support may reduce the co-operation and disclosure on which effective continuing risk assessment depends.*

(Grounds, 1995)

Laurance quotes a community psychiatrist:

> *. . . you can't eliminate risk in mental health work but you can move towards a system that people feel comfortable with, have trust in and where they feel you are on their side. And if you can make that happen, that is the safest service. You can have a measure with all sorts of restrictions and hurdles and safety measures but if the last person the user wants to see is the psychiatrist that is the least safe option.*

(Laurance, 2003)

In probation practice similarly, there is a questioning of the extent to which zealous enforcement fits with other probation objectives (Hedderman, 2003). In particular, Hearnden and Millie (2004) are unpersuaded that tougher and faster enforcement leads to a reduction in offending. They urge a shift in emphasis towards *securing* compliance, rather than a political emphasis on *demonstrating* it. This echoes the work of Bottoms whose analysis of mechanisms of compliance distinguishes (among other distinctions) instrumental and normative compliance (Bottoms, 2001). Instrumental compliance involves incentives and deterrents to which rational agents are expected to respond. Normative compliance emphasises *legitimacy*, recognising that people are more likely to meet demands and expectations that are – and are seen to be – reasonable and fair. Mere compulsion is a weak and temporary control: *legitimacy* is needed if active compliance is to be secured. These mechanisms of compliance must be made to work together.

Criminal justice and mental health research on compliance, then, both suggest that a reliance on instrumental compliance – amounting too often in practice to coercion and threat – is self-defeating. Disincentives to cooperation should be identified and, as far as possible, removed or mitigated; positive incentives to cooperate should be sought imaginatively. Above all, normative compliance must be secured and this can only be achieved where processes are fair and respect the individuality and legitimate interests of the person concerned.

Where there is a reluctance to take up service, this is interpreted as recalcitrance – for which the remedy must be 'enforcement' or compulsory treatment – rather than taken as a challenge to provide services that are seen by potential users as both accessible and relevant to them (DoH and Home Office, 2000b; Laurance, 2003). The point here is not just that this emphasis is oppressive and discriminatory (Kemshall, Canton and Bailey, forthcoming): it is also most unlikely to achieve compliance.

Moore astutely discusses the contribution that families, friends and carers might make to a risk management strategy (a contribution that, as Prins (1999) also emphasises, has too often been devalued):

. . . once they feel in control of at least part of a comprehensible process of supervision and protection.

(Moore, 1996)

This feeling will only be achieved where families are persuaded of the fairness of these processes of oversight, with respect for their interests and the interests of the patient.

Above all, this is a precondition for the active involvement of the subject of the risk plan: understanding and involvement of the individual in their own risk management is arguably the single most important component of any risk strategy. It is naïve, to be sure, to *depend* on this, to suppose that individuals will be consistently committed to avoiding offending or will have the insight to acknowledge and respond to increases in risk. But supposing that people can be policed effectively, against their will, or without regard to their reaction to the risk strategy centring upon them, represents naïveté of another kind. A risk plan, devised with the understanding and consent of the individual, should always be the aspiration. A purely actuarial assessment, seeing the individual as a bearer of risk factors, lacks legitimacy. By contrast, an assessment that takes proper account of the circumstances in which the individual has offended in the past, and links this assessment explicitly to a management plan, has the best chance of securing their compliance, and reducing risk.

References

Bhui, K. (1999) Cross cultural psychiatry and probation practice: a discourse on issues, context and practice. *Probation Journal.* 46: 2, 89–100.

Bhui, H.S. (2002) Probation in England and Wales: from rehabilitation to risk. *Journal of Forensic Psychiatry.* 13: 2, 231–9.

Blackburn, R. (2000) Classification and assessment of personality disorders: a psychological perspective. *Criminal Behaviour and Mental Health.* 10: S8–32.

Blumenthal, S. and Lavender, T. (2001) *Violence and Mental Disorder: A Critical Aid to the Assessment and Management of Risk.* London: Jessica Kingsley.

Bonta, J., Hanson, K., Law, M. (1998) The prediction of criminal and violent recidivism among mentally disordered offenders: a meta-analysis. *Psychological Bulletin.* 123: 2, 123–42.

Bottoms, A. (1995) The philosophy and politics of punishment and sentencing. In Chris Clarkson and Rod Morgan (Eds.) *The Politics of Sentencing Reform.* Oxford: Oxford University Press.

Bottoms, A. (2001) Compliance and community penalties. In Bottoms, A., Gelsthorpe, L. and Rex, S. (Eds.) *Community Penalties: Changes and Challenges.* Cullompton: Willan.

Brown, M. (2000) Calculations of risk in contemporary penal practice. In Brown, M. and Pratt, J. (Eds.) *Dangerous Offenders: Punishment And Social Order.* London: Routledge.

Busfield, J. (2002) Psychiatric disorder and individual violence: imagined death, risk and mental health policy. In Buchanan, A. (Ed.) *Care of the Mentally Disordered Offender in the Community.* Oxford: Oxford University Press.

Canton, R. (1995) Mental disorder, justice and censure. In Ward, D. and Lacey, M. (Eds.) *Probation: Working for Justice*, 1st edn. London: Whiting and Birch.

Canton, R. (2002) Rights, probation and mentally disturbed offenders. In Ward, D., Scott, J. and Lacey, M. (Eds.) *Probation: Working for Justice*, 2nd edn. Oxford: Oxford University Press.

Clark, D. (2003) Do all offenders benefit from programmes? *Criminal Justice Matters.* 52: 34–5.

Cohen, S. (1985) *Visions of Social Control.* Cambridge: Polity Press.

Cooke, D. (2000) *Current Risk Assessment Instruments. Annex 6 to the 'MacLean Report' A Report of the Committee on Serious Violent and Sexual Offenders.* Edinburgh: Scottish Executive.

Crisp, A. et al. (2000) The stigmatisation of people with mental illness. *British Journal of Psychiatry.* 177: 4–7.

Crichton, J. (Ed.) (1995) *Psychiatric Patient Violence: Risk and Response.* London: Duckworth.

Crichton, J. (1996) Psychiatric inpatient violence. In Walker, N. (Ed.) *Dangerous People.* London: Blackstone.

Crowe, M. and Carlyle, D. (2003) Deconstructing risk assessment and management in mental health nursing. *Journal of Advanced Nursing.* 43: 1, 19–27.

Dangerous and Severe Personality Disorder Programme (DSPD Programme) (accessed June 2004). *http://www.dspdprogramme.gov.uk/*

DoH and Home Office (2000a) *Reforming the Mental Health Act, Part One: The Legal Framework,* Cm 5016 I.

DoH and Home Office (2000b) *Reforming the Mental Health Act, Part Two: High Risk Patients,* Cm 5016 II.

Dolan, M. and Doyle, M. (2000) Violence risk prediction: clinical and actuarial measures and the role of the psychopathy checklist. *British Journal of Psychiatry.* 177: 303–11.

Fernando, S., Ndegwa, D. and Wilson, M. (1998) *Forensic Psychiatry, Race and Culture.* London: Routledge.

Garland, D. (2001) *The Culture of Control: Crime and Social Order in Contemporary Society.* Oxford: Oxford University Press.

Grounds, A. (1995) Risk assessment and management in clinical context. In Crichton, J. (Ed.) *Psychiatric Patient Violence: Risk and Relapse.* London: Duckworth.

Hannah-Moffat, K. (1999) Moral agent or actuarial subject: risk and Canadian women's imprisonment. *Theoretical Criminology.* 3: 1, 71–94.

Hearnden, I. and Millie, A. (2004) Does tougher enforcement lead to lower conviction? *Probation Journal.* 51: 1, 48–59.

Hedderman, C. (2003) Enforcing supervision and encouraging compliance. In Hong Chui, W. and Nellis, M. (Eds.) *Moving Probation Forward: Evidence, Arguments and Practice.* Harlow: Pearson Longman.

Hiroeh, U., Appleby, L., Mortensen, P. and Dunn, G. (2001) Death by homicide, suicide, and other unnatural causes in people with mental illness: a population-based study. *Lancet.* 358: 2110–2.

Hodgins, S. and Müller-Isberner, R. (Eds.) (2000) *Violence, Crime and Mentally Disordered Criminals: Concepts and Methods for Effective Treatment and Prevention.* Chichester: John Wiley.

Hodgins, S. (2004) Offenders with major mental disorders. In Hollin, C. (Ed.) *The Essential Handbook of Offender Assessment and Treatment*. Chichester: Wiley.

Jewesbury, I. and McCulloch, A. (2002) Public policy and mentally disordered offenders in the UK. In Buchanan, A. (Ed.) *Care of the Mentally Disordered Offender in the Community*. Oxford: Oxford University Press.

Kemshall, H. (2000) Conflicting knowledges on risk: the case of risk knowledge in the probation service. *Health, Risk and Society*. 2: 2, 143–58.

Kemshall, H. (2001) *Risk Assessment and Management of Known Sexual and Violent Offenders: A Review of Current Issues. Police Research Series Paper 140*. London: Home Office.

Kemshall, H. (2003) *Understanding Risk in Criminal Justice*. Maidenhead: Open University Press.

Kemshall, H. and Maguire, M. (2001) Public protection, partnership and risk penality: the multi-agency risk management of sexual and violent offenders. *Punishment and Society*. 3: 2, 237–64.

Kemshall, H., Canton, R. and Bailey, R. (forthcoming) *Dimensions of Difference*.

Laurance, J. (2003) *Pure Madness: How Fear Drives the Mental Health System*. London: Routledge.

Loader, I. and Sparks, R. (2002) Contemporary landscapes of crime, order and control: governance, risk and globalisation. In Maguire, M., Morgan, R. and Reiner, R. (Eds.) *The Oxford Handbook of Criminology*, 3rd edn. Oxford: Oxford University Press.

Lynch, M. (2000) Rehabilitation as rhetoric: the ideal of reformation in contemporary parole discourse and practices. *Punishment and Society*. 2: 1, 40–65.

Maguire, M., et al. (2001) *Risk Management of Sexual and Violent Offenders: The Work of Public Protection Panels, Police Research Series Paper 139*. London: Home Office.

McConville, M., Sanders, A. and Leng, R. (1991) *The Case for the Prosecution: Police Suspects and the Construction of Criminality*. London: Routledge.

McGuire, J. (2001) *Cognitive-Behavioural Approaches: An Introduction to Theory and Research*. London: Home Office.

McGuire, J. (2002) Multiple agencies with diverse goals. In Buchanan, A. (Ed.) *Care of the Mentally Disordered Offender in the Community*. Oxford: Oxford University Press.

Moore, B. (1996) *Risk Assessment: A Practitioner's Guide to Predicting Harmful Behaviour*. London: Whiting and Birch.

Morgan, S. (2000) *Clinical Risk Management: A Clinical Tool and Practitioner Manual*. London: Sainsbury Centre for Mental Health.

Mullen, P. (2002) Introduction to Buchanan, A. (Ed.) *Care of the Mentally Disordered Offender in the Community*. Oxford: Oxford University Press.

Munro, E. and Rumgay, J. (2000) Role of risk assessment in reducing homicides by people with mental illness. *British Journal of Psychiatry*. 176: 11–20.

National Confidential Inquiry (2001) *Safety First: Five Year Report of the National Confidential Inquiry into Suicide and Homicide by People with Mental Illness*. London: Stationery Office.

National Probation Service (2001) *A New Choreography: An Integrated Strategy for the National Probation Service for England and Wales*. London: Home Office.

Oldfield, M. (2002) *From Welfare to Risk: Discourse, Power and Politics in the Probation Service* (Issues in Community and Criminal Justice Monograph) London: National Association of Probation Officers.

Peay, J. (1982) 'Dangerousness' – ascription or description? In Feldman, P. (Ed.) *Developments in the Study of Criminal Behaviour. Volume 2: Violence*. Chichester: John Wiley.

Philo, G. (Ed.) (1996) *Media and Mental Distress*. London: Longman.

Porter, R. (2002) *Madness: A Brief History*. Oxford: Oxford University Press.

Potts, J. (1995) Risk assessment and management: a Home Office perspective. In Crichton, J. (Ed.) *Psychiatric Patient Violence: Risk and Response*. London: Duckworth.

Prins, H. (1995) *Offenders, Deviants or Patients?* 2nd edn, London: Routledge.

Prins, H. (1999) *Will They Do It Again? Risk Assessment and Management in Criminal Justice and Psychiatry*. London: Routledge.

Rack, P. (1982) *Race, Culture and Mental Disorder*. London: Tavistock.

Raynor, P. (2002) Community penalties: probation, punishment and 'what works'. In Maguire, M., Morgan, R. and Reiner, R. (Eds.) *The Oxford Handbook of Criminology*, 3rd edn. Oxford: Oxford University Press.

Raynor, P., Kinch, J., Roberts, C. and Merrington, S. (2000) *Risk and Need Assessment in Probation Services: An Evaluation. Home Office Research Study 211*. London: Home Office.

Ritchie, J., Dick, D. and Lingham, R. (1994) *The Report of the Inquiry Into the Care and Treatment of Christopher Clunis*. London: HMSO.

Robinson, G. (2001) Exploring risk management in probation practice: contemporary developments in England and Wales. *Punishment and Society*. 4: 1, 5–25.

Robinson, G. (2003) Risk and risk assessment. In Hong Chui, W. and Nellis, M. (Eds.) *Moving Probation Forward: Evidence, Arguments and Practice*. Harlow: Pearson Longman.

Rumgay, J. (2003) Partnerships in the probation service. In Hong Chui, W. and Nellis, M. (Eds.) *Moving Probation Forward: Evidence, Arguments and Practice*. Harlow: Pearson Longman.

Rumgay, J. and Munro, E. (2001) The lion's den: professional defences in the treatment of dangerous patients. *Journal of Forensic Psychiatry*. 12: 2, 357–78.

Scheff, T.J. (1984) *Being Mentally Ill: A Sociological Theory*, 2nd edn. New York: Aldine Publishing.

Scott, P. (1977) Assessing dangerousness in criminals. *British Journal of Psychiatry*. 131: 127–42.

Skeem, J. and Mulvey, E. (2002) Assessing the risk of violence posed by mentally disordered offenders being treated in the community. In Buchanan, A. (Ed.) *Care of the Mentally Disordered Offender in the Community*. Oxford: Oxford University Press.

Stephens, K. and Brown, I. (2001) OGRS2 In practice: an elastic ruler? *Probation Journal*. 48: 3, 179–87.

Tyrer, P. (2000) Improving the assessment of personality disorders. *Criminal Behaviour and Mental Health*. 10: S51–65.

Index